Humane, science-based horse training

Introduction to learning theory and exercises for everyday handling, care and fitness

Alizé Veillard-Muckensturm

Special thanks to Ceri Daugherty from www.subsidium.org.uk for proofreading this book. For editorial, financial and administrative services, please contact her at ceri@subsidium.org.uk or by telephone on 07814014286.

Thanks to Janneke Koekhoven from www.fedupfred.com for writing the foreword and creating the illustrations.

Thank you to Evelyne Veillard and Christopher Conway for their help with photographs.

First edition 2017
ISBN 978-1-9998363-0-6

Notice:
Horse care, training and riding is not without risk and while the author has made every effort to provide safe and accurate information to the best of their knowledge, this information is presented without any guarantee. Therefore, the author disclaims any liability incurred in connection to the information provided in this book.

For more on humane, science-based horse training visit www.fairhorsemanship.com

About this book

I started my equestrian journey as most people do. In a small riding school in France aged 8, I learned that to ride a horse you pull on the reins to stop, squeeze with your legs to go forward and if the horse does not cooperate, you give him a kick in the ribs or a smack behind your leg with your sparkly pink whip. I remember it not feeling like the right thing to do, after all I started riding lessons because I loved horses not because I wanted to hit them. But after a while, inflicting subtle punishment here and there after a refusal at a fence or a late canter start became normal and besides that it worked – the horse would eventually jump the fence or start cantering.

It was only when I got my own horses and therefore was no longer obligated to go to a riding club to spend time with my favourite animal that I started to look for a less confrontational way to ride. I spent many hours browsing the web, discussing on forums with others, and ordering and reading books. I started by removing their bits, then progressively stopped using my spurs and draw reins and no longer signed them up for show jumping or cross-country events. I found the old clicker I used to train my Jack Russell when he was a puppy and started introducing the use of food rewards in their everyday life. I initially started using it to teach them small 'tricks' such as to discriminate between two colours and then progressed to more 'serious' behaviours such as standing still for bathing. A few years down the line, I now use humane, science-based techniques for everything from health care procedures to fitness exercises and even riding.

I decided to write the book *Humane, science-based horse training* to help other horse lovers start a similar journey to mine towards a less confrontational, kinder relationship with their horses. This book will introduce you to the science behind animal training, answer your questions, and provide you with step by step training plans for twenty or so useful behaviours.

Have fun on your journey,

Alizé and the horses (Lyviera, Héros and Spirit)

Foreword by Janneke Koekhoven

"That horse is the last horse you should be giving food rewards to. It is unnatural and will teach your horse to bite and dominate you, mark my words!"

Sound familiar? It sure does to me. Do me a favour and pass this book onto those people once you finish. I can't believe I once talked like that myself back in the day. After asking for help from countless instructors and coaches, I ended up in a community very different from the horse world I had known from when I was little. I met Alizé in that community. She and others offered help and I remember being impressed by her online clicker training challenges, and all the videos the participants were sending in. She seemed like a very dedicated pioneer back then already. She was the one who urged me to do something more with my drawing tablet after I shared a little doodle of my own horse, which gave me the confidence to be a pioneer too and create Fred.

The world is always changing, slowly but surely, and for the better in my opinion. If you look at what was normal a mere 20 years ago (and examples tend to get more extreme as you look further back in time) that is not acceptable now, you know that we are still evolving. Racism, sexism, and now speciesism are more and more the subject of conversation. Somehow, horses seem to be a very special species. People tend to look down on others who train their horses "like they're dogs", when in fact horses are not that different from dogs. All animals learn the same way. If we can teach a rhino to stand on a scale, a goldfish to play soccer, a crocodile to ring a bell, a giraffe to give a blood sample, a cat to give high fives, then why would it be different for horses? Unfortunately, the horse world is about 20–30 years behind the dog training world but if someone is going to help give the horse world a nudge in the right direction, it's Alizé. She's a qualified horse behaviourist and trainer but much more importantly she's confident, smart, creative, eager to learn (and teach!), ethical, hardworking and very passionate about what she does. When she isn't going around giving lessons or speaking at seminars, Alizé is writing articles about humane, science-based horse training, making infographics with her own photography or animating videos for people to learn from, and share.

In my own way, I'm trying to contribute to this cause as much as I can. I've studied horses all my life and went through the classic phases of conventional, 'natural', and classical horsemanship before my horse finally forced me to look into humane, science-based horse training. We worked hard on the basics and now he'll load at liberty; park himself at the mounting block at liberty; put his own feet on the hoof stand for the trimmer; come when called; go on hacks, bike rides and walks with me; move on a circle; and rocks the agility ring at liberty. We're talking about a phlegmatic, reluctant, food aggressive, "dominant and lazy" labelled horse here. And I didn't even need a stick to make all that happen; I just needed to find a way to make him want to do it, instead of just doing it because I wanted it. Taking species-specific primary needs, emotions and abilities into account is key to humane, science-based horse training.

Years ago, I was lucky enough to get my hands on a proper book about reward based training; it was in my native language and mentioned some of the possibilities of clicker training without pressure-release. Suddenly, everything fell into place and

horse training became fun again. It warms my heart that this book will do the same
– and more – for people all over the world. The beautiful thing about humane,
science-based horse training is that once you see something, you can't unsee it. But I
promise you; you will love having a genuine two-way communication with your
horse. A horse who feels free to say "No", will say "Yes" in a way you've never
experienced before.

Janneke Koekhoven,
illustrator of 'Fed up Fred'.

What is humane, science-based horse training?

Humane, science-based horse training is a type of training where the trainer has learned, and continues to learn, about psychology and ethology and uses these for effective animal training. Furthermore, the training is ruled by ethics. This means that the trainer will not use harmful training techniques or make the animal perform physically or emotionally harmful behaviours exclusively for the sake of human convenience or entertainment.

The guiding principles of humane, science-based horse training are:

1. **Equine emotional and physical health.**

Before undergoing behavioural modification, pain should be ruled out as a factor by a veterinarian. The animal should be provided with regular and appropriate hoof care and dental care, and tack should be professionally checked to ensure comfort if riding is to take place.

Practices and devices which create fear and pain should not be used. These include the practice of abrupt, forced weaning; forced separation from herd mates; and the use of bits, whips, spurs and fixative tack.

2. **Species appropriate horse management.**

The horse should be provided with daily access to other horses, access to an enriched environment large enough to allow him freedom to act out most natural behaviours, and be fed a forage-based diet. Solitary confinement should be avoided as much as possible.

3. **Humane, science-based horse training.**

In case of unwanted or abnormal behaviour the horse health and management should first be assessed. Then, the least intrusive and most humane training techniques possible should be used.

Humane, science-based horse trainers primarily use antecedent arrangements, positive reinforcement, differential reinforcement, habituation, counter-conditioning and systematic desensitisation.

Negative reinforcement and punishments are avoided. The only exceptions are safety or emergency situations where no preferable alternatives are available.

Contents

Chapter 6: Trick training

Chapter 1
The science behind humane horse training

Before teaching new exercises to your horse and/or fixing behavioural problems, it is necessary to have a basic understanding of your horse's learning abilities. This chapter offers a brief overview of learning theory and principally focuses on explaining the techniques that follow humane, science-based principles.

1. Classical conditioning

During the 1890s, the psychologist Ivan Pavlov made an accidental discovery while studying the gastric system in dogs. He noticed that the dogs would start salivating whenever the researcher who fed the dogs entered the room. Fascinated by this finding, he conducted a series of experiments that led him to discover that any object or event could cause the dogs to salivate if they were associated with food. The type of learning displayed by Pavlov's dogs is now known as classical conditioning.

Classical conditioning is a type of associative learning in which a stimulus gains the capacity to evoke a response that was originally evoked by another stimulus. Both humans and non-humans can learn through classical conditioning.

Ivan Pavlov experiment:

Before learning	Before learning
Food = salivation	Sound of a bell = no response
During learning	**After learning**
Sound of a bell + food = salivation	Sound of a bell = salivation

Before conditioning takes place, the dogs would naturally salivate when they were presented with food. Salivation is an unconditioned response; animals do not need to learn how to salivate as it is a natural response to food. The food is an unconditioned stimulus, it naturally and automatically produces a response and in this case the response is salivation.

Before conditioning, the bell was a neutral stimulus; this means it was an object that produced no specific response in the dogs. The dogs would not salivate or do anything specific when the bell was rung.

During conditioning, the researcher would ring the bell and then give food to the dog; this would cause the dog to salivate. The process was repeated several times until the bell became a conditioned stimulus. A conditioned stimulus is a previously neutral stimulus that, after being associated with the unconditioned stimulus (in this example, food), triggers a conditioned response (salivation).

After conditioning took place the researcher could ring the bell and the dogs would salivate without the presence of food. Salivation here is a conditioned response; the dog had to learn to salivate at the sound of the bell during the conditioning phase as it is not a natural response.

Classical conditioning occurs all the time with horses. For example, horses can learn to associate the opening of the feed room with food, the halter with being caught for a ride, or a whip with the pain of being hit. While all these examples are about horses in the managed environment, classical conditioning also occurs with feral horses and is an important aspect of survival.

2. Operant conditioning

Operant conditioning (also known as Instrumental Learning) is a type of learning in which the individual's behaviour is shaped by consequences. It focuses on using reinforcement or punishment to increase or decrease behaviours. Through the process, an association is created between the behaviour and the consequence.

Psychologist Edward Thorndike was the first to study operant conditioning. He built puzzle boxes and placed a cat inside the box. The cat could only get out of the box and obtain a food reward by pressing the right latch. The cat would learn through trial and error what worked and what didn't.

Psychologist B.F. Skinner also studied operant conditioning and even published a book "The Behaviour of Organisms" on the subject. For his research, Skinner also designed a box in which animals such as rats and pigeons were exposed to stimuli and puzzles.

Just as with classical conditioning, both humans and non-human animals can learn through operant conditioning. Therefore, in this chapter we will give several examples of its application with humans as well as with non-human animals.

There are four quadrants of operant conditioning and we will look at each one in depth in this chapter but first let's quickly define all four of them.

- **Positive reinforcement** (+R) involves the addition of a pleasurable stimulus following a behaviour, making it more likely for this behaviour to occur again.

- **Negative reinforcement** (-R) involves the removal (or avoidance) of an aversive stimulus following a behaviour, making it more likely for this behaviour to occur again.

- **Positive punishment** (+P) involves the addition of an aversive stimulus following a behaviour, making it less likely for this behaviour to occur again.

- **Negative punishment** (-P) involves the removal of something desirable following a behaviour, making it less likely for this behaviour to occur again.

	Something is **added**	Something is **removed**
Increases the behaviour	Positive reinforcement	Negative reinforcement
Decreases the behaviour	Positive punishment	Negative punishment

The terms positive and negative are not a judgement of the technique; instead, positive means that something is added and negative means something is removed. Therefore, the term positive punishment does not mean "good punishment".

An important aspect of operant conditioning is that it is the learner who "decides" what contributes either reinforcement or punishment. Some horse owners tend to see reinforcers and punishers from their own point of view rather than that of their horse. So, for example, they think that because verbal praise is effective for them then it should be effective with their horses too. They do not take into account species differences.

Individual differences are also a factor. For example, a fearful horse may perceive a tap on the nose as positive punishment and therefore the behaviour the tap follows will decrease. But a playful horse may perceive a tap on the nose as positive reinforcement and an invitation to play and therefore the behaviour the tap follows will increase.

Operant conditioning occurs all the time even without our intervention. This free-ranging filly (on the right) left her mum's side to approach the young colt from another band. This behaviour is positively reinforced by play, making it more likely for her to approach the colt again in the future.

Conventional horse training

Mainstream types of horse training, including traditional and "natural" horsemanship, primarily involve the use of aversives. This means that typically, wanted behaviours are motivated through the use of negative reinforcement and unwanted behaviours are discouraged through the use of positive punishment.

Examples of negative reinforcement in horse training:

1. A rider kicks his horse's flanks to get him moving. When the horse starts moving, the rider reinforces the behaviour by removing the unpleasant stimulus (they stop kicking). The use of negative reinforcement makes it more likely for the horse to move forward again when cued to do so.

2. A rider pulls on the reins to stop his horse. When the horse stops, the rider reinforces the behaviour by removing the unpleasant stimulus (they stop pulling). The use of negative reinforcement makes it more likely for the horse to stop again when cued to do so.

Examples of positive punishment in horse training:

1. A rider whips his horse after he refuses to jump a fence. The rider punishes the horse by adding an aversive stimulus (being hit with a whip). The use of positive punishment makes it less likely for the horse to refuse jumping the fence again.

2. A rider yanks on his reins after his horse lowers his head down to try eating grass. The rider punishes the horse by adding an aversive stimulus (yanking). The use of positive punishment makes it less likely for the horse to try eating grass again.

While conventional horse training has many drawbacks, it generally works in making the horse do what we want as long as the aversive is taken off to reinforce the wanted behaviour (negative reinforcement). Often, horse riders experience problems while riding purely because they do not reinforce the wanted behaviour by taking the aversive off. For example, many people who complain that their horse is "lazy" spend nearly all their riding time squeezing and kicking their horse. This means that the horse is almost never reinforced for moving forward and therefore has little to no reason to do so. The same thing occurs with horses who are difficult to stop, often the riders do not remove the aversive (release the tension on the reins) when the horse performs the desired behaviour (slow down or stop).

3. Positive reinforcement

Positive reinforcement is at the heart of humane, science-based horse training, along with other non-coercive techniques such as habituation and appropriate horse management. Unfortunately, positive reinforcement is rarely used in the equestrian world; horses are primarily taught using a combination of negative reinforcement and positive punishment. However, it is commonly used in the dog-training world and also to handle wild and potentially dangerous animals such as hippopotamuses and lions.

Examples of positive reinforcement in the human world:

1. A child receives an A on his exam paper and to reward him his mum takes him to the cinema. Following the desired behaviour (good grades), the mother adds a pleasurable stimulus (going to cinema). The use of positive reinforcement makes it more likely for the child to work on getting good grades again.

2. A man does the laundry while his girlfriend has gone to the shop for groceries, when she comes back she thanks him and cooks a nice meal. Following the desired behaviour (doing the laundry), she adds a pleasurable stimulus (verbal praise +

food). The use of positive reinforcement makes it more likely for the man to take care of the laundry again.

Examples of positive reinforcement in animal training:

1. A dog gets a treat for sitting down on cue. The desired behaviour (sitting) is followed by a pleasurable stimulus (treat). The use of positive reinforcement makes it more likely for the dog to sit on cue again.

2. A zookeeper decides to teach a rhino to touch and follow the end of a stick in order to lead him onto a scale so he can monitor his weight. The zookeeper starts by presenting the stick and every time the rhino touches the stick with his nose he receives a treat. The desired behaviour (touching the stick) is followed by a pleasurable stimulus (treat). The use of positive reinforcement makes it more likely for the rhino to touch the stick and therefore makes it possible for the zookeeper to lure him onto the scale.

Benefits of positive reinforcement:

- **Create animals who choose to cooperate.** In conventional training, unpleasant stimuli are used to shape the animal's behaviour; these unpleasant stimuli create at least some discomfort, and at worst, pain. Positive reinforcement however, does not rely on making the animal fearful and uncomfortable; instead, it uses pleasant stimuli such as food and scratches to motivate wanted behaviour. This creates a non-fearful, happy, cooperative animal who can willingly participate in even uncomfortable healthcare procedures such as vaccinations, dental check-ups, blood tests, etc.

- **Motivation.** In 2008, Lesley Innes and Sebastian McBride conducted a study on a group of rescued equines to compare the use of negative reinforcement with the use of positive reinforcement in retraining. The results showed that the horses retrained with positive reinforcement were more willing to participate in training and displayed more explorative behaviours in novel situations.

- **Improve/maintain human/horse relationship.** Through the principle of classical conditioning, the human gets associated with positive stimuli which maintains or creates a positive human/horse relationship. The opposite is also true; when humans associate themselves with items or events that cause fear, discomfort, or pain, the relationship gets damaged.

  In 2010, a study was conducted on two groups of ponies to determine the effect of the type of reinforcement on the perception of humans by horses. Both groups were taught to back up on voice cue, one of the groups with positive reinforcement and the other with negative reinforcement. Negative reinforcement was associated with increased emotional state as indicated by both heart rate and behaviour (higher frequency of ears back and head movements), while positive reinforcement was associated with increased interest in the human. (Sankey et al., 2010)

- **Positive outlook on life.** Horses trained with rewards typically have what I call "a glass half full" perspective on life. They learn through training that new activities and objects usually bring rewards. So, when presented with something new and potentially scary, they tend to be less easily scared and more curious than the average horse who did not benefit from this training.

- **Focus.** While both negative reinforcement and positive reinforcement are effective in training new behaviours, negative reinforcement tends to work faster than positive reinforcement when it comes to training behaviours involving an element of flight, such as moving away from the trainer. It is however, less efficient when it comes to teaching nuanced, complex behaviours because the animal is primarily focused on escape rather than on puzzle solving.

- **True liberty.** With positive reinforcement, the horse wants to be with the human and wants to participate in the training session and therefore it is not uncommon for trainers to start a naïve horse at liberty. This is, however, not possible in conventional training; the trainer always has to start the training by using some kind of restriction such as a round pen or lead rope. It is only once the horse is trained and has learned that there is no escape, that he can be made to perform the movements without fences and ropes. While the horse looks at liberty, his mind is chained.

- **Aggression and depression.** The neurotransmitter known as dopamine is implicated in positive reinforcement because it plays a role in reinforcing the behaviour by making the animal feel good. This also leads to an increase in serotonin. Low serotonin is not only linked to depression but also to low CSF 5-HIAA, which in turn is associated with risk taking behaviour (including aggression) and distorted thinking.

- **Enrichment.** Training based on the use of positive reinforcement is a great way to stimulate and enrich the life of the domesticated horse. Enrichment not only provides mental and physical exercise, but it can also help reduce or eliminate abnormal behaviours such as stereotypies (crib-biting, weaving etc.) when used alongside species-appropriate management.

Disadvantages of positive reinforcement

When compared to other quadrants of operant conditioning, positive reinforcement does not have many disadvantages. However, you will occasionally hear about horse owners who have abandoned the idea of using positive reinforcement after their horses became increasingly frustrated and/or aggressive when trained with food rewards.

While this does not always happen, unwanted behaviours and unwanted emotional states may arise when using rewards with horses if the training is done incorrectly or is not personalised to fit the individual horse. The main reason for this is that the handler possesses something the animal desires and the horse is tempted to steal, or gets frustrated because he is prevented from accessing it.

Horses who are the most at risk include those who have been starved in the past, and horses with novice handlers who have no professional guidance and therefore end up making mistakes. In this book, we will look at how this problem can be prevented and how it can be dealt with if already occurring.

Contrary to popular belief, the practice of hand feeding horses does not create nipping and biting behaviours. In 2010, researchers Jo Hockenhull and Emma Creighton investigated unwanted oral investigative behaviour in horses during hand feeding. They found that 91% of the horses in the study displayed at least one oral investigative behaviours (such as hand licking) but no nipping or biting. Nipping and biting originated from another source than hand feeding.

The risk of accidental negative punishment

As noted previously, negative punishment involves the removal of something desirable following a behaviour. Because, with positive reinforcement, you work with stimuli that the horse desires such as food and scratches, it is easy to accidentally punish the horse.

For example, horses may perceive sudden breaks during training sessions as negative punishment. When you stop to take a phone call or have a discussion with someone, you remove the horse's opportunity to earn treats or scratches. Therefore, it is essential to give your full attention to the horse during the training session and to establish an end of session ritual that you can use when finishing the session or taking a break. Typically, this is done by putting a handful of treats on the floor and removing the treat bag so the horse learns not to expect any more treats from this point on.

Unethical use of positive reinforcement

Positive reinforcement is the most humane quadrant of operant conditioning to use in animal training, however, it can still be used in unethical ways. How? Typically, this is done using a high value reward that outweighs the negative consequences of doing the behaviour. For example, positive reinforcement can be used to train a horse with back pain to stand still at the mounting block using a food item that the horse particularly enjoys.

In addition, the trainer is likely to control the environment in order to limit the horse's choices and make the wanted behaviour (e.g. standing by the mounting block) more likely to happen. This may include; not feeding the horse outside the training session, keeping the horse on a lead, or keeping them in a barren environment with nothing else to do.

Entertainment parks that use wild animals such as orcas are a good example of unethical use of positive reinforcement. The animals are kept in environments that do not meet their needs and the training sessions are, more often than not, their only source of enrichment. While it is better for these animals to be trained using positive reinforcement than other methods, one cannot label such training as ethical.

The science of how animals learn can easily be used as a weapon against the animal to make him perform damaging behaviours. This is possible with positive reinforcement just as much as with the other quadrants of operant conditioning.

Hence, this book is not simply titled "Science-based horse training" but "Humane, science-based horse training". Ethics is just as much part of this training philosophy as the science.

"But you cannot use positive reinforcement all the time!"

Every time I hear this I have a picture that comes to mind: a small boat going in the direction of four drowning people. One of the people on the rescue boat says "But we only have space for three" and so the boat turns around and all four drown.

While yes there are times where you may find yourself having to use negative reinforcement or even positive punishment on a horse, this however, does not mean that you shouldn't aim to use the least amount of aversives possible when around horses. Committing to do so is crucial if you want to do the best for your animal.

More importantly, you should ask yourself if the reason why you are considering using aversives is truly fair to the horse. Are you using them in an emergency situation where there are no suitable alternatives? Or is it because you would like the horse to do something that is fun or convenient for you more than it is for him?

4. Habituation

Habituation is known as the simplest form of learning; both humans and non-human animals can learn through habituation, this includes more "simple life forms" such as snails.

With habituation, the individual's original response to a stimulus decreases after repeated presentations. This means that if a horse is initially afraid of, let's say, cars, his fear will progressively reduce as he sees more and more vehicles drive past his field. As the fear decreases, the behavioural response to the stimuli decreases too. At first, the horse may run all the way to the bottom of his field but after a few cars have driven past, he may start to run less or just raise his head until finally he continues grazing no matter how many cars pass by.

This type of learning does not require any reinforcement or the involvement of the trainer and therefore is quite easy to use. For example, to habituate a horse to a trailer/horse box, you can park it in his field and let the horse learn on his own. Of course, when doing this it is essential to think about where you are placing the potentially threatening stimulus; it shouldn't prevent the horse from accessing important resources such as water and shouldn't block the animal's escape routes.

Flooding is often mislabelled as habituation by horse trainers. However, flooding can be defined as the repeated presentation of a fear-provoking stimulus in a context where the individual cannot escape. So, for example, chasing the horse with a tarp while the animal is stuck in an enclosure such as a round- pen, small arena or stall, or on a lead rope.

Flooding is not habituation. For habituation to be successful, the stimulus that is considered threatening needs not to cause any harm to the animal or the fear will be reinforced. Flooding causes brain fatigue and the horse may become highly phobic or shut down.

These free-ranging ponies habituate to vehicles from an early age as hundreds of cars pass through their home range on a daily basis.

5. Systematic desensitisation

Systematic desensitisation is a training technique that consists of exposing the animal to a weaker version of an aversive stimulus in order to increase his tolerance to it. It is a powerful tool in the treatment of phobias both for humans and non-human animals. The technique can be used with either habituation or counter conditioning.

Systematic desensitisation is different to habituation; with habituation, the animal is exposed to the full version of the stimulus rather than a weakened version. Because of this, systematic desensitisation is more suitable than habituation when it comes to learned-fears.

A weaker version of the stimulus can be created by:

- **Breaking the stimulus into small components.** For example, if a horse bolts when meeting running and barking dogs, he could first be introduced to a small quiet dog who remains seated. Movement and sound can be added later on in the training.

- **Using distance.** The fear-provoking stimulus can be presented at a distance that significantly reduces the fear response. The ideal distance is where the horse only displays alert signals rather than fear or aggression signals.

6. Counter Conditioning

Counter conditioning is a classical conditioning process that can be used to change the animal's response to a stimulus by associating this stimulus with one of opposite value. It is used on both humans and non-human animals in the treatment of fears, anxiety, phobias and even aggression.

So, for example, if a horse has developed a fear of dogs due to being bitten by one, the trainer can give treats to the horse every time he sees a dog. The treats create a pleasant emotional response that works to drive the stimulus (dog) value towards neutral.

Counter conditioning is often used with systematic desensitisation. This is because it is difficult to create a positive association in an animal who is actively experiencing fear. With desensitisation, counter conditioning occurs when the individual is exposed to a weaker version of his fear.

Evelyne uses both counter-conditioning and systematic desensitisation to desensitise Lyviera to umbrellas. At first, the umbrella is presented in its closed form and then progressively opened. She will then work on additional elements such as the position of the umbrella, or the sound of the rain on the it to best prepare the mare for a real-life situation.

Chapter 2
Training your horse humanely and scientifically

In the first chapter, you were introduced to some basic learning theory; now it is time to dig a little deeper and learn how to apply this knowledge to train your horse.

1. The trainer's toolbox

THE CLICKER

As clicker training has become quite popular amount dog owners, you are likely to find a clicker for purchase at your local pet store.

A clicker is a small noisemaker that produces a distinctive clicking sound when pressed. The clicking sound is also known as a "bridge" because it creates a bridge between the desired behaviour and the delivery of the reward. The purpose of the clicker is to improve timing, to enable you to precisely mark the moment your horse offered the desired behaviour so he knows what earned him a reinforcer.

Just as you can give any meaning you like to a clicker (after all it's only a little clicking box!) you can use practically anything as a bridge signal. For example, dolphin trainers use whistles and fish owners use flashlights. If your horse is deaf, you can even use a hand signal or a touch as a bridge signal.

The horse learns the meaning of the clicker through classical conditioning:

Before learning	Before learning
Food = feel good	Clicking sound = no response
During learning	**After learning**
Clicking sound + food = feel good	Clicking sound = feel good

For some horses, the clicking sound produced by the clicker is not a neutral stimulus to start with and instead the horse shows fear when hearing the click. If this is the case with your horse, you can either muffle the sound by putting the clicker in your pocket or try using the click of a ballpoint pen.

In some situations, holding a clicker is unpractical; this is when you may want to use a verbal bridge. A verbal bridge can be a single distinct word such as "bing", "right", "ya", or a sound you make with your mouth such as a tongue click or a whistle. When choosing a verbal bridge, it is important to not choose something you or other people may accidently say to your horse such as "good boy".

Verbal bridge or clicker?

In 2007, Lindsay Wood conducted a study on two groups of naïve dogs to find out if there was any difference between using a verbal bridge signal (the word "yes") and a clicker. Both groups were taught the same behaviour of bumping a target with their nose; only the bridge signal was different. The dogs in the clicker group completed the training faster (on average 36 minutes) than the dogs in the verbal bridge group (on average 59 minutes). These results can be explained by the fact that the clicker, unlike a spoken word, is a completely new and neutral stimulus. The clicker also makes the exact same noise every time whereas the spoken word can vary in tone and volume.

Using an intermediate bridge

More often than not, the clicker is used as what we call a terminal bridge. It not only tells the horse "that's right!" but also marks the end of the behaviour and tells the animal that a reward is coming.

But what if we are working on a longer task such as completing an obstacle course and cannot stop after every fence to reward the horse? How can I tell my horse he is on the right track without giving him a click and a treat? This is where an intermediate bridge may be useful. An intermediate bridge marks successful moments advancing toward the complete behaviour; it means "that's right, keep going!".

It is commonly used in training patrol dogs to keep searching for a lost item and can be used with horses, for example, to encourage a horse to maintain canter for a few more strides or to keep their leg up for the farrier.

To teach a "keep going" signal to your horse, first select a sound or a word that is different to your terminal bridge signal and simply start inserting it into your training, preferably with behaviours that the horse already knows and that involve some kind of duration such as standing still, lunging etc. The animal will soon learn its meaning and the intermediate bridge will become a useful tool in your training.

REINFORCERS

Reinforcers are essential in motivating behaviour; they increase the likelihood that a specific behaviour will occur. There are negative reinforcers, used with negative reinforcement; and there are positive reinforcers, used with positive reinforcement.

In addition, there are two main types of reinforcers; primary reinforcers and secondary reinforcers. Primary reinforcers do not need to be learned, they have an innate biological value and typically relate to the basic needs of the animal. Food, water and sex are all example of positive primary reinforcers.

Secondary reinforcers (also called conditioned reinforcers) are learned through association with primary reinforcers; and predict reinforcement. A human example of a secondary reinforcer is money. We work hard to gain money, but only do so because we can exchange it for things that we desire or need such as food, water, shelter etc. If all of sudden nobody would take our money, then it would stop being reinforcing and we wouldn't work to earn it.

In humane, science-based training the clicker is an example of a secondary reinforcer; after being associated with food or/and scratches several times it becomes a predictor for reinforcement.

Targets and cues can also be considered secondary reinforcers; although they are sometimes called tertiary reinforcers to better describe how far removed they are from the primary reinforcer.

TARGETS

Targets are objects that your horse can learn to touch and follow with different parts of his body. Anything can be used as a target as long as it is safe; no sharp edges and no object that is small enough for the horse to swallow. Old whips can be recycled into targets by placing an object such as a tennis ball on the end of them. Telescopic fly swatters and small cones also make good targets.

Targets are useful to move the horse, or any part of his body, without the use of aversive pressure and can help you train desired behaviours without strain such as trailer loading or lunging.

BUM BAG

A bum bag has two purposes. Not only can it hold food rewards but it can also be a great discriminative stimulus that can let your horse know when training is available.

By simply putting it on when you are training and not bringing it when you just want to hang out, your horse will learn to recognise when he has the opportunity to earn reinforcers. This allows the horse to relax in your presence and not to feel the need to offer his entire behaviour repertoire every time he sees you, which risks frustration at the lack of rewards.

If you do not want to use your bum bag as a discriminative stimulus, you may use anything else you want that will stand out to your horse such as a neck rope, a cap, a jacket etc.

PROTECTED CONTACT

With some animals, you may temporarily wish to work behind protective contact such as a gate or a stable door. While positive reinforcement is less dangerous for the trainer than negative reinforcement, many animals have experienced prejudice in the past and may react in a dangerous manner. For example, some horses may push or try to bite their trainer.

Even if the horse is calm, it is still a good idea to start naïve horses behind protective contact to teach them the basics: stand still and calm, and targeting. If all goes well you can then work with them in full contact.

Protective contact is not only for beginners and even experienced trainers use it. It is not only about staying safe but also about setting up the horse for success. A horse who may be struggling to learn to stand calm and still in full contact, may learn the skill in only a few minutes when taught behind protective contact as there is less room for errors. For example, the horse won't be able to circle around the trainer.

Protective contact is also a powerful tool in training humans to handle animals confidently and effectively. The barrier guarantees a certain security to the person and because the person feels safe they can then do a much better job.

2. Techniques to obtain desired behaviours

I come from a conventional horse training background where I was taught that there was only one technique to obtain desired behaviours in horses; negative reinforcement. Of course, my instructors didn't know about learning theory so they would label it as "pressure/release" or "put your legs on until he does it". The words would change from one person to the next but in the end it was always the same thing. All of this changed when I learned about positive reinforcement. I was shocked to find that there was more than one way of doing things; in fact there were 7 different techniques you could use to teach a desired behaviour to an animal. These are: capturing, luring, targeting, moulding, free shaping, mimicry and aversive stimulation.

This section offers a quick overview of all 7 techniques; we will learn a lot more about them as we see them (except for aversive stimulation) being used in practice in the training plans.

CAPTURING

Capturing is what most people picture when you mention positive reinforcement or clicker training: A trainer with a clicker and treats at the ready, waiting patiently for their animal to do something they may want to reinforce.

While the technique does require the trainer to wait for the behaviour to occur and then click and reward, it isn't usually as time consuming as it sounds. For example, if a trainer wants to teach his horse to lie down on cue he will start by setting up the stage so the horse is likely to want to roll. This may involve turning the horse out in the sand arena or giving the horse a bath first. When the animal goes to roll, the trainer can then click and reward the horse with a treat.

Capturing is extremely useful if the trainer wants to get difficult behaviours such as yawning or urinating on cue. It is also an amazing tool to encourage good posture and beautiful movement in the horse. For example, when playing or being lunged, a horse may naturally exhibit collected paces that can easily be reinforced (and therefore made more likely to occur again) with a click followed by a treat.

FREE SHAPING

Free shaping is similar to capturing, but instead of capturing the wanted behaviour, the trainer captures the small steps the horse offers that head towards the desired behaviour. The trainer progressively raises the criteria for reinforcement in order to get closer to the goal behaviour; this means the animal will have to do a little bit more than he did on his previous try to earn the reinforcer. Eventually the trainer gets the full desired behaviour and can work on putting it on cue.

Free shaping is useful in getting an animal to do extremely complex and precise behaviours without strain; but it is not an easy technique for beginners to use as the animal can become confused and/or frustrated if not reinforced when necessary or if the criteria is raised too quickly.

MOULDING

Moulding, also known as sculpting, involves physically moving the animal into a desired position. Moulding should be used with caution as it may involve aversive stimulation. For example, if a trainer has previously taught his horse to pick up his legs using negative reinforcement and then proceeds to use moulding to teach the horse to place his feet on a hoof cradle, the situation is likely to be unpleasant to the horse.

Moulding can be useful in some situations such as teaching a horse to place a foot on a hoof cradle for hoof care procedures, but the trainer should be aware of the horse's history and pay close attention to the animal's body language in order to determine what motivates the compliance.

LURING

Luring consists of moving the animal into a desired position or location using a pleasurable stimulus – usually food. It is not rare to see conventional horse riders using this technique to try to convince their horse to load in a trailer to go to the show.

Luring can be useful especially with horses who haven't received training yet; a bucket of food can be used to convince a horse to load into a trailer or to bring escaped horses back to safety.

Luring is less efficient than other techniques as the animal primarily focuses on the food rather than on the task. Its applications are limited as the animal can only be moved by following the lure with his nose; parts of the body such as shoulders or hips cannot be lured individually, unlike with targeting.

TARGETING

Targeting is similar to luring except that the animal does not follow a food item but a target and can follow this target more than just with their nose. A horse can target with a knee, shoulder, hip, hoof and many more. Targeting can be useful for many different behaviours including husbandry behaviours such as leading, giving feet, health care procedures (such as using an inhaler or administrating wormer), and even for schooling such as going over a jump or moving the shoulders.

Héros following a target stick – a recycled whip with a
tennis ball at the end of it – over some raised poles.

MIMICRY

Mimicry consists of showing – or having another animal demonstrate – the desired
behaviour and then reinforcing it. This technique hasn't really been explored with
horses yet and until recently, all studies conducted on social learning in horses
produced no significant evidence of such learning. However, the results may have
been influenced by the experimental conditions and trial designs. For example, in
Clarke et al.'s (1996) study, the demonstrator was an unfamiliar horse who was only
stabled next door to the other horses (test subjects) for a period of 18 hours prior to
the experiment. This was almost certainly an insufficient time for familiarisation.

In 2013, Krueger conducted a social experiment with 30 socially kept horses of
different ages, breeds and gender. The herds all had a stable hierarchy for at least 2
years prior to the experiment, making them highly familiar with each other.

5 middle ranking horses of average age were trained to be demonstrators; they
learned to pull a rope on an experimental apparatus which opened a drawer that
contained food. The other 25 horses individually observed 1 of the demonstrators
operating the apparatus and eating the food. The demonstrator was then taken away
and the observer was left with the apparatus.

12 horses successfully opened the drawer following demonstration. They were all
significantly younger than the demonstrator horse and were younger, lower in rank,
and displayed more exploratory behaviour than the horses who were unsuccessful.
Krueger suggests that older horses won't follow the example of younger horses as
they may make mistakes and eat dangerous food.

So, horses can learn from each other but can they learn from us? In another social learning study, humans were used as demonstrators. The study involved 24 horses; 12 of the horses observed a familiar person opening an apparatus containing food while the other 12 did not receive any demonstration. 8 of the 12 horses in the demonstration group successfully learned to operate the apparatus while only 2 of the 12 horses in the no-demonstration group managed it.

The results suggest that yes, horses can learn socially across species and therefore social learning may be an efficient and humane horse training technique; however, cues can sometime be confused with mimicry. For example, one popular cue for the Spanish walk is the trainer lifting his legs up while standing near the horse. At first glance the horse appears to mimic the trainer but the behaviour was initially learned using another technique such as targeting or aversive stimulation.

AVERSIVE STIMULATION

Desired behaviours can also be produced through negative reinforcement and this is the conventional way of obtaining them; the trainer introduces an aversive stimulus and then removes it when the horse performs the desired behaviour in order to reinforce it.

Sometimes, the trainer may first use negative reinforcement and when the animal does the desired behaviour they present a food reward. The problem with this technique is that the horse's behaviour is first motivated by an aversive and then a pleasurable stimulus is added. We can argue that this is not an example of positive reinforcement because it's not the addition of a pleasurable stimuli that reinforces the behaviour and makes it more likely to occur again in the future, but the removal of an aversive.

Effects of mixing negative reinforcement and positive reinforcement

In 2007, Nicole Murrey conducted a series of experiments in which she investigated the differences between using both types of reinforcement, or positive reinforcement only to train a dog. During the experiments, one behaviour was taught in two conditions with two different cues. In the first condition, the dog was given a cue and then the leash was pulled to prompt the behaviour and a reward was delivered (mixed reinforcement). In the second condition, the dog was given a cue and then rewarded for successive approximation towards the goal behaviour.

Both techniques were effective; however, the dog's responses were more accurate during the positive reinforcement only condition and most errors occurred during the mixed reinforcement condition. The most significant difference between the two conditions was the emotional behaviour; high tail wags occurred in most trials in the positive reinforcement only condition, while low tail wags would mostly occur in the mixed reinforcement condition.

This last finding brings out a very important point; one of the benefits of positive reinforcement is that it creates a happy and willing animal, but by mixing reinforcement the horse may find himself in a less preferable emotional state. Because we have other techniques available such as shaping, targeting etc. that do not require any aversives, mixing reinforcement is usually not necessary and is best kept for the odd emergency situation.

3. Reinforce behaviours

Some equestrians are uneasy with the idea of giving food rewards to their horses; not only because of the few horror stories and myths being spread around, but also because they would like horses to do things because they want to, for us, rather than for a treat. One of the issues with this romantic idea is that it completely ignores learning theory. It assumes that in conventional training horses jump, compete and do canter pirouettes over and over again for fun rather than because they have learned to do so through the use of negative reinforcement and positive punishment.

If you want your horse to reliably perform behaviours then you have no choice, you need to provide him with some sort of extrinsic motivation – a reason for him to act out the behaviour you want at the time you want – rather than doing something else or nothing. And there are only two ways to do that; either you use fear/discomfort or you use rewards such as food and scratches. This section will teach you a little bit more about the use of positive reinforcers and how they can be progressively faded out without losing reliability.

Scratches can be used to reinforce desired behaviour, to build a positive association with touch and to soothe a threatened horse.

HOW TO CHOOSE THE RIGHT REINFORCER FOR YOUR HORSE

Horses can have their behaviour positively reinforced in many ways, but during a training session the choices of primary reinforcers are limited to food and scratches. However, not all reinforcers have the same value and what can work well as a reward for one horse may be ineffective for another.

There are 3 main factors that can impact upon the value of a reinforcer:

- **Individual differences.** Reinforcers are not all equal in value and the value of the reward depends on the individual. One horse may find pieces of carrots highly reinforcing, while another may have no interest in them and prefers apples slices.

- **The environment.** The environment can affect the value of a reinforcer. Once the environment is modified, a horse who once worked well to earn a specific reinforcer may no longer be motivated by it.

  For example, a trainer starts working with a riding club horse who is stabled 23/7 and gets very good results exclusively using scratches to motivate behaviours. After a few weeks of training, he decides to buy this horse and starts to keep him in the field with his other horses. He finds out that scratches do not work very well as reward anymore with this horse. Scratches that once used to be high value rewards for this horse are now low value rewards. What happened? The environment has changed. The horse is now kept in an environment that allows him to fulfil his scratching needs (trees, mutual grooming with other horses) and therefore scratches are not as salient anymore.

- **History.** Past experiences may affect the value of a reinforcer. Many horses suffer (or have suffered) from forage restriction and, as a consequence, their seeking system is highly activated. For some of these horses, food has become "too important", causing over-arousal, biting, mugging and other undesirable behaviour. More importantly, these horses are simply not happy while training regardless of food being involved.

When getting started with humane, science-based training it is a good idea to first try commonly low/medium value reinforcers such as haylage, chaff, celery, scratches and high fibre pony cubes. If necessary, you can then work your way up to reinforcers that are usually more valued by horses such as carrots, apples and sweet feed.

You can also use higher value rewards to reinforce the most difficult tasks and behaviours, or your horse's best efforts. Carrying two types of treats is a good idea, so if your horse does something particularly well and with a lot of enthusiasm, you can deliver the higher value reward instead of his usual reward.

EXTRINSIC AND INSTRINSIC MOTIVATION

A horse's motivation to perform a specific behaviour can arise from within or from the outside. Extrinsic motivation is the type of motivation most often seen in the equestrian world. The horse is motivated to perform a behaviour to remove an unpleasant stimulus (negative reinforcement), to gain access to a pleasurable stimulus (positive reinforcement), or to avoid punishment. Examples of extrinsic motivation in the human world include studying to avoid getting detention or going to work to earn money.

Intrinsic motivation is the opposite; the horse or human engages in a specific behaviour because the behaviour is rewarding in itself. Horses playing in the field with each other and jumping a ditch once in a while out of their own free will do it because they enjoy the activity for its own sake. Examples of intrinsic motivation in the human world include solving puzzles or participating in a sport.

External rewards are useful tools that can be used to induce interest in something the horse had no initial interest in, such as giving his hooves for hoof care or accepting medication. They can also be used to teach the skills necessary for the activity to potentially become more intrinsically motivating and less extrinsically motivating. Potential examples of this include teaching a horse to play with a ball or teaching a horse to go out of the yard for walk in the countryside. External rewards are also important in motivating the individual to perform a specific behaviour at a specific time and for a set amount of time, something that is often necessary in animal care and training.

SCHEDULES OF REINFORCEMENT

Reinforcement schedules are rules that dictate when (and how often) a behaviour is reinforced. Reinforcement schedules are used in both positive reinforcement and negative reinforcement. Choosing the right schedule of reinforcement for the behaviour – and the horse – is essential as it dictates the rate at which the horse learns and how quickly he responds to cues.

There are 5 main types of reinforcement schedules:

- **Continuous reinforcement schedule.** The desired response is reinforced every single time it occurs. For example, the horse receives a food reward every time he picks up his leg or puts on his headcollar. The main advantage of using a continuous reinforcement schedule is that learning occurs quickly and therefore, this is the best schedule to choose when introducing a horse to a new exercise. However, because the horse is reinforced every single time it can be time consuming and unpractical in the long term; which is one of the reasons that once the horse starts to understand the exercise, trainers typically switch to a different schedule of reinforcement. Satiation is another disadvantage of using a continuous schedule; because the animal receives the reward every single time he can quickly become full and uninterested.

- **Fixed ratio schedule.** The horse is reinforced after a fixed number of correct responses. For example, a horse receives a food reward every 4 fences he jumps. This schedule can cause the horse to pause for a significant amount of time after receiving reinforcement as he realises that he must perform the same behaviour another x amount of times before achieving reinforcement. It can also cause the horse to make less effort for the jumps he knows won't be reinforced and to rush through them.

- **Variable ratio schedule.** The number of correct responses that are reinforced varies; there is no fix pattern of reinforcement. For example, a horse receives a food reward after 5 strides of canter and the next time after 12 strides of canter. This schedule is not efficient in teaching new behaviours but is ideal to maintain an already learned behaviour. The horse doesn't pause after receiving the reward because he has learned that he may have to offer fewer responses to achieve reinforcement

- **Fixed interval schedules.** The horse is reinforced for the first behaviour performed after a fix amount of time. For example, a horse on a hack is reinforced with a food reward for trotting every 60 seconds. While it is easy to implement, the horse can figure out the schedule and only begin to trot when reinforcement is due.

- **Variable interval schedules.** The time when the horse is reinforced varies. For example, a horse receives a food reward after trotting for 20 seconds and the next time after trotting for 30 seconds. This schedule has similar drawbacks and advantages to a variable ratio schedule.

One concern many people have when starting using rewards in training is that if they start to do so then they will always have to feed the horse for every single thing. Thankfully this is not true. Typically, the horse is first taught the wanted behaviour on a continuous reinforcement schedule before being moved to a variable schedule of reinforcement. So, for example, if you are teaching a young horse to walk over raised poles you start by rewarding him every time he goes over a pole (continuous reinforcement schedule). Once he understands what is required you can switch to a different schedule of reinforcement and progressively ask the horse to step over more and more poles before obtaining reinforcement.

BEHAVIOUR CHAINS

A behaviour chain is a sequence of individual behaviours that are linked together by cues. One of the advantages of creating behaviour chains is that once each individual behaviour has been taught you no longer need to reinforce each of them with a primary reinforcer (such as food); instead you can use the cue as a secondary reinforcer for the next behaviour in the chain.

Each cue in the behaviour chain is perceived as an opportunity to earn something desirable and therefore is perceived as a rewarding event by the horse.

Examples of behaviour chains:

1. Night-feeding behaviour chain: A groom calls out to a horse who is turned out in a field, the horse comes when hearing his name and lowers his head to allow the groom to put on his headcollar. He then follows the groom all the way to his stable where he receives his evening feed.

In this scenario, the horse performs a chain of 3 behaviours (come when called, lower head when presented with headcollar and follow groom) and at the end of the chain is rewarded with food. However, the individual behaviours are not rewarded with food but by receiving the next cue in the chain.

2. Going for a ride behaviour chain: A rider presents a horse with his bridle and the horse lowers his head into it. The horse then stands still while the rider places the saddle on his back. The rider opens the stable door and the horse follows the rider into the arena. The rider climbs on the mounting block and the horse comes to line up beside it. The rider gets on and gives a treat to her horse.

In this scenario, the horse performs a chain of 4 behaviours (lower head into bridle, stand still for saddle, follow rider to the arena, line up to mounting block) and at the end of the chain is rewarded with a food reward.

REAL LIFE REWARDS

Once a horse has learned a desired behaviour this behaviour can be maintained through real-life rewards. For example, once a horse has learned to put on a headcollar successfully, the handler can fade out the use of food reward and let the desired behaviour be maintained by naturally occurring positive consequences such as being led to the field for turnout time.

Once the horse has learned to follow and willingly leave his herd-mate(s) behind, you can use real-life rewards such as browsing opportunities to reinforce him and maintain his desire to go out for walks or rides.

4. Shaping behaviours

Shaping (also known as successive approximation) is a method that consists of breaking down the goal behaviour into small steps and reinforcing the horse for completing these small steps that eventually lead him to performing the goal behaviour.

Shaping does not replace the need for reinforcement and the desired response can be generated using techniques such as luring and targeting – unlike free-shaping where the response is spontaneous.

A behaviour such as walking calmly alongside a person underneath an umbrella requires the use of shaping. First, the handler teaches the horse to walk alongside her – perhaps using a target. Once the horse starts to understand the behaviour the target is faded out. Some horses may benefit from additional steps such as learning to walk alongside their handler while the handler has a hand raised. Afterwards the handler desensitises the horse to the umbrella, first presenting it closed and then opening it progressively so as not to scare the mare. Once the horse is comfortable with the object he can be desensitised to other elements such as movement and position. The last step is to teach the horse to lead in the presence of the umbrella, something that is now rather simple as the horse is not afraid of it and already knows how to lead.

Examples of shaping in the human world:

1. When children first learn to ride a bike, they are typically assisted by stabilisers (training wheels) that help them to keep their balance while they learn to pedal and use the brakes. When the child has had enough practice, the stabilisers are removed and replaced by the close supervision of an adult who typically prevents the child from falling by holding their shoulders. Eventually, the child learns to pedal with no assistance and is then capable of going on longer rides.

2. Writing is one of the best examples of shaping in the human world. At first, the young child learns to hold the pen properly and to retrace letters that have been written in faint lines or using spots. Once the child has learned to write the letters he progresses to writing numbers and words. Guides such as feint lines and spots are removed progressively. The child learns to copy small sentences and eventually to make his own. The process goes on as the child learns to write paragraphs and then essays.

Now what would happen if we asked a small child to ride a bike for the first time with no assistance whatsoever and another to write a full paragraph without prior training? Well, both would probably give up pretty quickly as they couldn't gain reinforcement and the first one would probably injure himself and not want to sit on a bike ever again. This is what we too often do to horses – most often without knowing – we ask them to complete very difficult tasks with little to no preparation and often get upset when they don't succeed when we are the ones forgetting the importance of shaping.

Tips to successfully shape a behaviour:

- First determine your goal behaviour.

- Write down the small easy steps that lead towards your goal behaviour. In shaping, one of the most common reasons for training failure is the lack of small steps.

- Use the shaping plan you have written as a guide during training but remain flexible. Some animals may require smaller steps than others, while some may jump steps. Stay ahead of your animal to avoid frustration and keep training fun.

- Shape one aspect of the behaviour at a time and relax your other criteria while working on a specific aspect of the behaviour. For example, relax your criteria for duration while working on generalisation. If you have successfully taught your horse to give and hold his hoof up for 10 seconds at a time and now want to introduce him to doing the same with a different person, do not ask him to give his hoof plus hold it for 10 seconds on his first trial.

- Read shaping plans written by other trainers and watch videos showing shaping plans being implemented.

5. Putting behaviours on cue

Putting a behaviour on cue as a humane, science-based horse trainer is a very different experience than putting a behaviour on cue as a mainstream horse trainer. In conventional horse training, there is little to no discussion on the subject of "putting behaviours on cue" and this is because the trainer nearly always starts with the cue. For example, if a rider is teaching a young horse to walk forward, he will start by squeezing the animal's flanks with his leg and escalate this pressure until the horse finds it aversive enough to try to escape it, typically by moving forward. Once the horse moves the trainer stops squeezing/kicking. After a few repetitions, the horse perceives the squeeze of the legs as his opportunity to avoid more unpleasant pressure and walks on when the rider starts squeezing. The leg pressure is both how the trainer got the horse to perform the wanted behaviour and the cue.

In humane, science-based training, many times we capture the behaviour or free shape the behaviour which means that we do not start with a cue and therefore, once we have got the behaviour we want, we still have to put it on cue. This can be done in a few ways.

Methods to put a behaviour on cue:

1. You can give the cue while the behaviour is starting and then reinforce the behaviour when completed. After some repetition, you should be able to put the cue before the behaviour and have the animal respond to the cue by doing the desired behaviour.

2. You can train a cue like you would train behaviour. Give the animal the cue and click the animal's first movement towards doing the behaviour. After some repetition, you can go back to bridging for the complete behaviour.

In some cases, the horse learns the behaviour and the cue at the same time. This is the case for behaviours taught using targeting, where the presentation of the target in a specific position becomes a cue. In these cases, it is possible to change the cue to something else such as a verbal word, a touch, or a sign.

Example of how to change a cue:

A rider has taught his horse to back up several steps using targeting and food rewards, but would like to fade out the use of target and have his horse back up on a verbal cue so the behaviour can be used for lunging and riding. To do so he uses the principle of classical conditioning as shown below.

Before learning	Before learning
Position of the target = back up	"Back up" = no response
During learning	**After learning**
"Back up" + target = back up	"Back up" = back up

He starts by saying "back up", waits a second before presenting the target in the usual position and the horse starts backing up. He clicks and rewards the horse for backing up, repeating the process several times. After a number of repetitions the horse starts responding by making a timid step back after he says "back up" and before he presents the target. From there he shapes the cue the same way he would shape a behaviour; by reinforcing the little steps the horse is making. After some more training the horse responses by backing up every time he hears "back up".

6. Keeping it positive

Despite our best efforts, using positive reinforcement does not necessarily guarantee that the horse will have a good time during training. Compared to negative reinforcement, positive reinforcement has few drawbacks but over-arousal and frustration may occur in some horses. And while this is not an issue that all newcomers to positive reinforcement may face, it can discourage many. Thankfully, the problem can be eliminated with appropriate horse management, training adjustment and patience.

BODY LANGUAGE

Taking pictures of your horse is a good way to get to know what stress looks like for him. The above picture was taken when a new horse was introduced to the herd and threatened Lyviera. Her neck is raised and tense, her nostril flared, there is tension above her eyes, and her ears are listening to the other horses' movements. Her fear becomes even more obvious when we compare it to a picture of her at rest (below).

Regardless of the training method used, you can obtain information on a horse's emotional state by looking at his body language and behaviour in a holistic way. It is essential to look at the whole horse – as well as the context – when gathering information because some signs can have several meanings. For example, a frightened, anxious horse can hold his ears backwards, laterally and even forwards. This is because ears don't only indicate the animal's emotional state; they also help to gather information and therefore can indicate what the horse is listening/paying attention to.

When animals are faced with a potential threat they have 4 behavioural options at their disposal. They can fight, flee, freeze, and/or fiddle about; and some species such as hognose snakes have a fifth option "faint". Typically, all healthy animals will react to a relatively low risk threat by fiddling about or freezing and most will choose flight over fight unless escape is prevented.

Behaviours that fall under the fiddling about categories include; displacement behaviours, which are normal behaviours occurring out of their normal context, and appeasement behaviours, which are submissive behaviours that are designed to reduce aggression levels in an aggressor. These are also referred to as calming signals. Recognising these behaviours is important as they give you the chance to adjust the environment and training before the stressor(s) seriously compromise the horse's welfare and your safety.

Examples of appeasement and displacement behaviours:

- Pawing the ground
- Head tossing
- Lip licking
- Empty chewing
- Yawning
- Turning the neck/head away from the trainer
- Sniffing the ground/seeking out distractions
- Scratching self
- Fiddling on the spot
- Slow movement

As mentioned before, it is important to look at the context in which these behaviours occur and at the rest of the horse's body language as some of these behaviours (e.g. yawning) can occur without the presence of a perceived threat.

Additional signs to watch for when training a horse include:

- Ears fixed backwards
- Narrowing of the eyes
- Overall muscle tension
- Raised, tense neck
- Tense mouth and pronounced chin or a long nose
- Flared or pinched nostrils
- Snatching or grabbing at the food
- Nipping the trainer
- Freezing

- Submissive posture: head lowered and unresponsive to stimuli apart from handler/trainer commands
- Redirected aggression
- Dropping/erection of the penis

Regarding this last point, it is worth mentioning that at present, no scientific studies have been published on the topic of erections and dropping in clicker training. While we know that dropping, erections and masturbation – even without the presence of a mare – is normal male horse behaviour, it typically occurs at rest rather than in a training context. From personal observation, erections and dropping in training seem to mostly occur alongside other signs of mild stress.

WHEN POSITIVE TRAINING BECOMES NEGATIVE

There are a number of situations during which your attempt at using humane, science-based methods may not bring you the desired results. A horse may experience conflict when you are using positive reinforcement in the following situations:

- During a training session which includes both negative and positive reinforcement or if you are using a cue that has been taught using aversives and now click/treat the horse's response to the cue.

- During a training session where the horse is rewarded for desired responses (positive reinforcement) but punished for undesirable responses (positive punishment). For example, the horse is given a treat for standing still and straight but tapped on the nose for sniffing the handler.

- During a training session where the handler uses negative punishment by, for example, removing his attention and therefore his horse's opportunity to earn a desired reward rather than using more humane options such as teaching an incompatible behaviour or changing the environment to limit the odds of the unwanted behaviour occurring.

- The environment or handler has become "poisoned" due to being associated with aversive training or experiences in the past, making the horse anxious regardless of the use of food.

- When the horse is required to perform a behaviour he is not completely comfortable with but feels compelled to try it to earn reinforcement. This may include behaviours that are frightening or painful to the horse or too physically demanding for the horse's fitness level.

- When the horse is struggling with impulse control; his desire to get to the food and not being able to get to it.

- When the horse feels threatened by the proximity of other horses or the possibility of losing desired resources such as food and his handler to the other horses. Remember, just because you believe that you are far enough away from the other horses, it does not mean that your horse necessarily feels the same way. Comfortable distances may also vary depending on the horse. Horses will feel less threatened by the presence of their pair-bond than the presence of a random horse.

- When the horse is taken away from the rest of the herd but is not completely comfortable with this separation.

- When the horse has experienced starvation in the past. Starvation being any feeding regime that regularly does not allow the horse to forage at least 16 hours a day. Ideally, horses should be provided with 24/7 access to forage.

MAKING IT POSITIVE AGAIN

First, establish which of the above situations may apply to your horse. Once you have established what causes stress to your horse the solution may be obvious. For example, if mixing the quadrants is a factor, remove your use of negative reinforcement and punishment from the session, learn alternative ways to deal with unwanted behaviours and teach new cues with positive reinforcement.

If your horse has a resource guarding issue or has suffered from starvation in the past, there are additional things you can do besides training at a distance from the other horses such as:

- Evaluate your horse's nutritional needs and meet them.

- If applicable, stabilise the horse's weight and fix deficiencies before starting training with food rewards again.

- Make sure the horse has eaten prior to training so he is not being trained in a state of hunger.

- Always start the training when the horse is calm and not performing any unwanted behaviour.

- Trial different reinforcers and use one which has a lower/medium value. Typically, haylage, high fibre nuts and chaff are lower in value than sweet feed and apples but it does depend on the individual horse.

- Experiment with the quantity of the reinforcer; a handful of food rather than teaspoon quantity may help the horse to calm down as he gains satisfaction from chewing.

- Try using a higher rate of reinforcement.

- You can also lower the value of a reinforcer by making it available outside the training sessions using treat-balls or by scattering it on his hay. This way, the reinforcer will not be perceived as a scarce resource.

Another situation that must be addressed in more detail is when the handler or environment has become a conditioned stimulus due to unpleasant past experiences; thereby provoking a negative conditioned emotional response (of fear/rage). In these cases, the most important thing to do is to no longer pair the environment and the handler with events that provoke fear, discomfort or pain. In the case of the handler, stop all training and riding temporarily and start a process of desensitisation where the handler spends time with the horse doing close to nothing except sharing space while letting the horse engage in whatever activity he wishes. The idea is to break the pattern of your presence or arrival always meaning something somewhat unpleasant will occur.

Once the horse no longer shows undesired body language or behaviours, food (other than forage) can be reintroduced in your presence using puzzles. Make sure the puzzles are not too complex for your horse so he doesn't experience frustration. If the horse is calm you can then reintroduce short training sessions, doing very simple tasks, exclusively involving humane, science-based training techniques.

Some horses new to targeting show signs of fear/rage when asked to back up or move their hindquarters toward a target stick. One possible explanation for this is that the target looks too much like a whip when combined with the position required to create backward or hip movements and therefore causes some fear. Try switching to a different target – such as a small cone – and see if that makes a difference to the horse's emotional state.

7. Techniques to deal with unwanted behaviours

There are 3 necessary steps to deal with your horse's unwanted behaviour humanely. First, always rule out pain by consulting a qualified veterinarian. Sometimes a check-up may be enough to rule out any physical problem but you may need to get other equine professionals involved such as the dentist, chiropractor or saddle fitter.

If you ignore this advice and try solving something that is not a behavioural issue with some training, one day or another your horse will collapse – either physically or emotionally – and you may get injured in the process.

Many behavioural problems such as aggression and stereotypies (also known as 'stable vices') can be avoided, reduced or eliminated by providing horses with companionship, freedom of movement and a forage based diet.

Secondly, try to understand why the horse would act in such manner. Avoid negative and anthropomorphic thinking such as "he is just doing it to annoy me" or "he is just being silly". Such thoughts predispose you to think of punishment rather than finding a compassionate solution.

Instead try to answer questions such as:

- How is the behaviour reinforced? Look at what consequences follow the unwanted behaviour.

- Is there a pattern to the unwanted behaviour? When does it occur and how often? Try to identify what caused the unwanted behaviour to occur in the first place.

- Is my horse's behaviour caused by past history/trauma? A horse may be particularly fearful of a situation or an object because it has been associated with unpleasant consequences in the past. For example, horses who have been food deprived in the past may be more prone to being food aggressive.

- Is my current management fulfilling the key needs of my horse? A horse may be depressed, aggressive or difficult to manage because his needs are not being met.

- Can the unwanted behaviour be explained by ethology? Horses are social animals who feel safe when in a herd so, for example, it is not unreasonable for a horse to be reluctant to leave others behind if he hasn't been properly prepared to do so.

Once you have an understanding of the problem, you can choose one (or several) of the techniques explained in this section to reduce or/and eliminate the unwanted behaviour. Always choose the least intrusive solution possible and primarily focus on eliminating the reason for the behaviour rather than the behaviour itself.

ANTECEDENT ARRANGEMENT

Antecedent arrangement consists of looking at the problem in terms of antecedent, behaviour and consequence, and rearranging the environment to prevent the behaviour from occurring in the first place.

The antecedent is what happens immediately before the unwanted behaviour and is what gets the ball rolling. The consequence is what happens immediately after the behaviour and reinforces it, thereby making it more likely to occur again.

Let's look at some unwanted behaviour in terms of antecedent, behaviour and consequence and see how antecedent arrangement can be used in these scenarios.

Scenario 1: Every time Cynthia wants to feed her horses she opens the door of the feed room to prepare the food. Every time her horse, Beauty, sees Cynthia opening the door she starts to bang on her stable door and paws the ground vigorously; only stopping once she has received her food.

Antecedent	Behaviour	Consequence
The feed room door	Pawing	Food

Through classical conditioning, Beauty has learnt to associate the feed room door with food and starts pawing the ground in excitement. Cynthia positively reinforces the pawing behaviour by always giving the food to Beauty.

In this scenario, antecedent arrangement would involve avoiding the pawing occurring in the first place by, for example, changing the location of the feed room (preferably out of sight) or by preparing Beauty's feed in advance so she would no longer associate the feed room door with food.

It is also important to note that pawing can be a sign of stress and over-arousal and therefore it may indicate that Beauty does not benefit from appropriate horse management. For example, Beauty may be fed too little forage and have spent several hours without food before being given a concentrated feed. The behaviour may not have occurred in the first place if Beauty was allowed to eat a forage based diet 16 to 18 hours a day as horses have evolved to do.

<u>Scenario 2:</u> Carol's horse, Oliver, frequently puts his tongue over the bit while being ridden. This causes Carol to feel unsafe and to have difficulties directing Oliver's movements.

Antecedent	Behaviour	Consequence
Bitted bridle	Putting tongue over the bit	Relief from the bit

Conventional horse riders often use a bit (metal device placed in the horse mouth) to control their horse's movements, alongside their use of negative reinforcement and positive punishment. Most bits have a port or joint that digs into the horse's palate when pressure is applied. Some horses have found that putting their tongue over the bit alleviates the pain.

In this scenario, antecedent arrangement would involve removing the bit and swapping for a bit-less bridle – this way, Oliver not only cannot pass his tongue over the bit but also does not need to. The bit-less bridle will allow Oliver to be more comfortable even if Carol rides in a conventional way.

Carol should also ensure that the bit did not damage Oliver's tongue, mouth and teeth by consulting a qualified equine dentist.

REDIRECTION

Sometimes, unwanted behaviours are simply natural behaviour. For example, a cat may jump on furniture, a dog may chew your shoes and a horse may scratch on fragile fencing. Cats naturally seek out high places so they can survey their territory and feel safe, dogs chew to keep their jaw strong and teeth clean and horses particularly enjoy a good scratch.

In these cases, it serves no purpose to try to remove the behaviour and you can redirect the natural behaviour towards more appropriate surfaces instead. Get the cat a couple of cat trees, the dog some toys and bones, and the horse both a friend for mutual grooming and a scratching post for self-grooming.

SYSTEMATIC DESENSITISATION AND COUNTER CONDITIONING

Sometimes, a horse may have received treatment for a physical issue but still displays unwanted behaviour. For example, a horse who has been treated for a sore back may still try to avoid the saddle. This is because the saddle has been associated with pain through the process of classical conditioning.

Before learning	Before learning
Sore back = pain	Saddle = no pain
During learning	**After learning**
Saddle + Sore back = pain	Saddle = pain

Because the saddle has been associated with pain, seeing the saddle will cause fear to the horse. Flooding the horse and just strapping the saddle on his back without his consent won't stop the horse from trying to avoid the saddle next time because while there is no longer any pain, the fear is very much alive.

Combining systematic desensitisation and counter conditioning is an effective and humane solution to reduce the horse's fear and remove the unwanted behaviour, as long as the pain issue has been resolved.

In this example, using systematic desensitisation will consist of breaking the saddling process down into small components, starting by simply reducing the horse's response to seeing the saddle. When the horse no longer reacts fearfully to seeing the saddle, the trainer can move to the next step by moving the saddle towards the horse's body. The process continues like this until the horse can be saddled.

Counter conditioning can be used alongside systematic desensitisation to help speed up the process and change the horse's emotional response to the saddle by associating it with a pleasurable stimulus such as food.

Before learning	Before learning
Saddle = pain	Treats = feel good
During learning	**After learning**
Saddle + treats = feel good	Saddle = feel good

TEACHING AN INCOMPATIBLE BEHAVIOUR

This technique doesn't involve addressing the antecedent and therefore should only be used after the horse's health and management has been assessed. It involves using positive reinforcement to teach the animal a behaviour that is incompatible with the unwanted behaviour; instead of punishing the horse for what we do not want, we teach him what we would like.

Examples of uses of incompatible behaviours:

1. If a horse has a habit of searching your pockets for food you can teach him to stand still with his head facing forward instead. The horse cannot do both behaviours at the same time; because you also stop reinforcing the pocket searching and start reinforcing the standing still and calm behaviour, the horse learns to do the latter instead.

2. It is common for horses to stand in groups by the gate of the field; this makes taking only one horse out difficult and even dangerous. A good solution to this problem is to teach each horse to go to a target when you approach the gate.

EXTINCTION

Extinction refers to the gradual decrease of a behaviour. In classical conditioning, it occurs when a conditioned stimulus ceases to be paired with an unconditioned stimulus and therefore progressively ceases to elicit a conditioned response. Remember Ivan Pavlov's experiment discussed in the first chapter? If the bell stops being paired with the food, the dogs will eventually stop salivating when hearing the bell.

In operant conditioning, it occurs when a learned behaviour is no longer reinforced. For example, a horse who has previously learned to push a treat-ball to earn food, will progressively stop doing if the owner no longer fills it (and therefore the ball no longer produces food) as the horse learns that pushing the ball does not achieve anything.

At first, the behaviour may get worse before getting better and this is known as an extinction burst. The behaviour will increase in intensity as the animal tries to make it work. So, for example, a horse who has been taught to lift his leg up to get a cookie may try to lift it up even higher which can be quite dangerous for the handler.

Extinction is a gradual process, during which there are risks of spontaneous recovery episodes where the behaviour may reoccur but at a lower intensity than originally.

Extinction should be used carefully and preferably not on its own as it can easily cause "extinction-induced depression" or frustration due to the loss of reward. For example, to teach a horse to no longer search his owner's pockets, the handler will do their best to stop reinforcing the unwanted behaviour (extinction) but also reinforce an incompatible behaviour. This way, we can prevent the horse from becoming frustrated or depressed. Behaviours that have been associated with extinction-induced depression in animals include avoidance of site of reward and biting and rearing behaviour (Huston et al, 2013).

Extinction is often mistaken for negative punishment. Here are a few points to help you spot the difference:

- Extinction can occur with both operantly conditioned and classically conditioned behaviours. Negative punishment is a quadrant of operant conditioning.

- Unlike negative punishment, extinction involves no postcedent change in the environment. Negative punishment is an event, extinction is a non-event.

- Extinction eliminates behaviours by removing all reinforcers; unlike negative punishment that merely superimposes a punisher (removal of a desired/pleasurable stimuli) over any reinforcers.

PUNISHMENT

Punishment, everyone's favourite way of dealing with unwanted behaviour yet the worst option of them all. As mentioned in the first chapter of this book, there are two types of punishment; negative punishment and positive punishment.

Positive punishment involves the addition of an aversive stimulus following a behaviour, thereby making it less likely for this behaviour to occur again. Negative punishment, however, involves the removal of something desirable following a behaviour, thereby making it less likely for this behaviour to occur again.

Drawbacks of punishment:

- **Encourages avoidance instead of willing cooperation.** An animal who has learned that a specific situation frequently leads to punishment will develop a desire to avoid the situation altogether. This is also true for humans; for example, a child living with punishing parents may start to spend more time away from home, run away or lie to avoid punishment. In the equestrian world, it is not rare for horses to become really difficult to catch when turned out as they have associated being caught with punishing situations such as being ridden with aversives or locked in a stable with little to nothing to do.

- **Unwanted associations.** Through classical conditioning the horse forms associations between stimuli; punishments can be associated with people, places or items that were present when the punishments occurred. This can cause the horse to exhibit even more unwanted behaviours. For example, if a horse has learned that he is often punished in the riding arena he may refuse to enter it.

- **Aggression.** Punishment increases the risk of aggression and therefore is a safety hazard. The individual may react to the pain and/or fear by attacking the aggressor or redirect his aggression to whatever else is around. For example, a horse may nip his owner or handler's hand during a painful veterinarian procedure or attack a nearby horse when ridden in a punishing way.

A 2009 study performed on dogs by Dr Megan Herron, found that the more severe the punishment was the more likely the dog was to react aggressively. For example, 43% of dogs who were hit or kicked reacted aggressively while only 15% reacted aggressively when shouted 'no' at them. However, it is worth mentioning that it is the individual who experiences the punishment who decides how aversive it is; some animals may find being shouted at way more aversive than others. Therefore, it is important when looking at punishment to avoid thoughts such as "it was only a small smack" because the lens through which we perceive the punishment we administer is different than the one of the horse who receives it.

- **Chronic stress.** Chronic stress occurs when an individual is repeatedly exposed to stressors for an extended period of time. Animals who are routinely exposed to punishment are at risk of developing chronic stress. Unlike acute stress that can be beneficial to our survival, chronic stress has many undesirable effects. The elevated level of cortisol compromises the immune system, making animals suffering from chronic stress more prone to diseases and take longer to recover from illnesses.

In the equestrian world, chronic stress tends to be overlooked as the anxiety it causes tends to be wrongly attributed to personality or breed. The result is most often a horse who suffers in silence.

- **Effectiveness.** A 2004 study conducted on dogs compared reward-based training methods (positive reinforcement) with punishment-based training methods and found that punishment was less effective (Hiby et al., 2004). The dogs who were rewarded had less occurrence of over-excitement, less separation related problems and were reported to be more obedient.

- **It doesn't address the cause of the unwanted behaviour.** One reason why punishment can be ineffective is because it does not address the cause of the problem, it simply adds an aversive stimulus (positive punishment) or removes something desirable (negative punishment). It does not address the antecedent or remove the reinforcement for the behaviour. This may cause mild punishment to be completely ineffective, leading the trainer to use more painful, more threatening punishment in order to override the reinforcement provided by the unwanted behaviour. This can cause punishment to become not just an ethical issue, but a welfare issue, especially if the unwanted behaviour is caused by pain.

Is there really a place for punishment in modern animal training?

Most people will probably say yes and a few years ago, I would probably have said the same. Now, looking at the array of techniques available to deal with unwanted behaviour, I find punishment not only unnecessary but also too costly because of all the drawbacks mentioned above. We do not need our horses to be battle ready or to put bread on the table, we use them primarily for fun and companionship. We have the time to learn and use alternative techniques.

In humane, science-based horse training, punishment should be reserved for the rare emergency situations where there is no other option to keep yourself and/or your horse safe. This way, punishment is used to protect. But, what you may have to do during an emergency shouldn't be what you do in training. Once the danger has passed the trainer must then prevent the unwanted behaviour from occurring again using humane, science-based hose training methods rather than relying on the use of punishment.

8. Troubleshooting: When your horse just won't do it!

In this section, we are going to look at some of the different factors that can affect your horse's rate of learning and cause the horse to not perform, or perform unreliably.

SALIENCY

Saliency refers to the level to which a stimulus can catch and retain an individual's interest. The saliency of a stimulus varies depending on the species, the individual's history, personal preferences etc. For example, a toy is likely to have a high saliency for a child but low saliency for an adult. It is unlikely you will motivate an adult to perform a task by rewarding him with a toy, but you are likely to be successful in getting a child to perform tasks if toys are used as rewards.

When working with horses you want to make sure you use rewards that are sufficiently salient to motivate wanted behaviours. Food has high saliency and scratches have typically lower saliency than food. Different food types have different saliency, typically chaff and hay have low saliency and carrots and sweet feed have high saliency.

CONTIGUITY

Learning rate is also influenced by contiguity, which means learning takes place only if events occur relatively close together in time. A horse is more likely to learn (and will learn faster) if the consequence happens as, or very soon after, the animal performs the behaviour. This is why you always want to try to deliver the reinforcement as quickly as possible during, or following, the desired behaviour; if you are unable to do this you can use a bridge signal such as a clicker to improve contiguity.

Contiguity is just as important in the case of classical conditioning. If you want your horse to learn to perform a behaviour that once only followed an unconditioned stimulus in response to the presentation of a neutral stimulus, you need to closely associate the neutral stimulus and the unconditioned stimulus together.

Pavlov would have had a hard time teaching his dogs to salivate to the sound of a bell (see chapter 1, section 1) if he had waited an extended period of time before presenting them with the food once he had rung the bell. The dogs may have not have learned to salivate to the sound of the bell or would have taken considerably longer to train.

Poor contiguity can lead to the animal learning superstitious behaviours. The animal develops superstitious behaviours by making connections between unrelated stimuli because of their accidental contiguity with a reinforcer. For example, a horse owner wants to teach her horse to stop nicely by her shoulder every time she stops walking. When the horse stops, the owner takes a while to retrieve one of the pieces of carrots, when she finally gets it out the horse is busy scratching his front leg so she waits and give him the carrot as soon as he is done. The scenario repeats itself a few times and just like that the horse has developed a superstitious behaviour and always go to scratch his leg every time they stop. To fix this, the horse owner will need to start reinforcing the horse as soon as he stops and before he has the time to lower his head all the way to his leg.

FREQUENCY

In some cases, stimuli are so salient that they do not require rehearsal to find their way to long-term memory. For example, a dog may become a conditioned stimulus to a horse and provoke a conditioned emotional response of fear if a dog seriously injured the horse on their first meeting.

But in most cases, you will have to regularly train and do a few repetitions per training session to consolidate learning. Think of it this way, you wouldn't have learned your times tables on the first read, so why expect your horse to do so?

OVERSHADOWING

Overshadowing occurs when two or more stimuli are presented at the same time but one is more salient than the other. For example, a horse may ignore the target and dive for the grass when you first start training with positive reinforcement. In this scenario, the grass is more salient to the horse than the target and this is why the horse won't touch the target with his nose when presented with the opportunity. One way to solve such a problem is to first introduce your horse to target training in an environment with few distractions and build a strong reinforcement history so the target become more salient. While doing this, you can reduce the saliency of the grass by giving him access to it outside the training sessions so he no longer perceives it as a scarce resource. And while it may sound impossible, with training the target can eventually overshadow the grass!

Overshadowing also occurs with aversive stimuli. For example, a horse who injured himself while being travelled in a trailer is likely to become fearful of them and become difficult to load. Depending on the horse, the target may be more salient than the trailer and the horse will load by following it or the trailer will be more salient than the target and the horse will refuse to load.

In conventional horse training, the trainer typically combats this problem by being more salient (scarier) than the trailer. This is of course not ethical and won't remove the fear. Instead, it is recommended to reduce the horse's fear of the trailer using counter conditioning and systematic desensitisation.

PREPAREDNESS

Different species have different behaviours that they are more prepared to learn about than others due to them already being part of their natural ethogram. For example, it is relatively easy to teach a dog to dig on cue or a crow to pick up a shiny object. Similarly, some behaviours are difficult to teach because they are not part of the animal's natural ethogram and/or go against the animal's natural instincts. So, if you want to teach a horse to load and travel a trailer or to leave his herd behind, you will have to be a lot more patient than if you are teaching him to follow another horse or touch an object with his nose, both of which are natural equine behaviours.

TRIGGER STACKING

Trigger stacking happens when multiple stressors or stressful events occur at the same time or relatively close together. When stressors are combined, they can cause the animal to go over threshold of reactivity and act out flight or fight behaviours. A horse over threshold won't be able to focus and learn a new task.

One way to deal with trigger stacking is to learn to recognise subtle signs of stress, work to reduce the animal's stress and not add additional stressors. Signs of stress include, but are not limited to; licking and chewing, flared nostrils, alertness, raised head and tense neck, tight mouth and pronounced chin etc. It is important for the trainer to dedicate time to desensitise his horse to common stressors such as vehicles, people, dogs etc. to reduce the chances of trigger stacking occurring. Appropriate horse management will help avoid stress brought on by a low forage diet, lack of freedom of movement and social isolation.

Example of trigger stacking:

A horse owner wants to go for a ride on a rainy day, unfortunately nobody else on the yard wants to accompany her so she saddles her horse and leaves the yard. As she is riding along a bridle path a man opens his umbrella and her horse bolts with her.

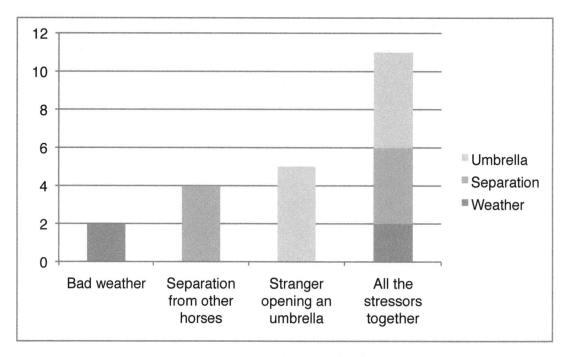

Each stressor has his own value to the horse and when stacked together they cause the horse to go over his threshold of reactivity (10) and attempt to escape.

After this unpleasant experience the owner decides to use counter conditioning and systematic desensitisation to lower her horse's reactivity to these stressors. A month later she decides to go on a ride on another rainy day; the same circumstances are present but this time her horse is more relaxed and does not bolt.

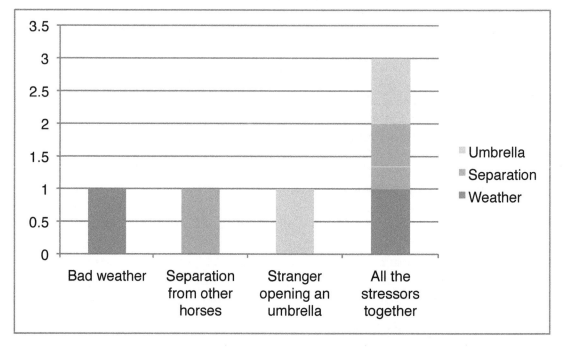

GENERALISATION

"I know he can do it, he did it just fine at home!" says a frustrated horse rider trying to get her horse to load in a trailer at a show. Most likely, the rider has trained her horse to load and unload several times on the yard so she could bring him to the show, but did not spend time training in other locations with added distractions so the horse hasn't generalised the trailer loading skill.

Generalisation occurs when an individual responds to a new (yet similar) stimulus in the same way as he did with a previously encountered stimulus. For example, we know that 20 and 7569 are both numbers and that a Labrador and a Jack Russell are both dogs.

The human equivalent of skipping the generalisation step in training would be, for example, to teach you to drive a small car in an empty parking lot and then expect you to drive a large 4x4 in the middle of New York city. Good luck with that! To avoid causing your horse to have a breakdown in the equine equivalent of New York city, you must progressively get him used to performing the behaviour of your choice in different environments and with added distractions.

Héros performing the Spanish walk in the forestry. When outside the yard, I typically start with a lower than usually criteria for example: 1 or 2 steps leads to reinforcement rather than 3 or 4. I then adjust my criteria depending on the horse's response, emotional state and on any distractions that may come along such as a person walking by with his dog off the lead.

Chapter 3
Foundation training

To get the best results the exercises presented in this section should be completed before moving on to any other exercises presented in later chapters. In addition, the handler should have read the previous chapters, or at the very least, chapter 2 of this book.

1. Carrying out a successful training session

Before calling your horse over for his training session, make sure you are prepared. Interruptions during training can be perceived as negative punishment by the horse (as you are removing something desirable) and can cause frustration. Therefore, make sure you won't be interrupted, turn your phone off if you must and make sure you have more reinforcers than necessary so you won't run out and have to leave your horse behind to go get more.

Your first training session doesn't have to be longer than 5 minutes. With undivided attention and a solid plan in mind a lot can be achieved in a short amount of time. Later on, the length of the training sessions can be adjusted to fit horse and handler; some horses can benefit from regular but short sessions of 2 minutes while others can be trained for 20 minutes at a time without losing focus or motivation.

Always start the training session when the horse is calm and has had the opportunity to act out most of his natural behaviours. This means it is preferable to train a horse who has had the opportunity to forage, have social interactions with other horses and the possibility to move freely.

Never start the training session if the horse is performing unwanted behaviours such as pawing and is in a negative emotional state. The training sessions are positive reinforcers due to involving food and/or scratches and therefore, if you start the session when the horse is performing unwanted behaviours, you are reinforcing these behaviours.

Preferably use a discriminative stimulus that indicates to the horse when reward-based training is available and when it isn't. This can be done by putting on a bum bag for training and removing it when the session end.

Always quit when you are ahead, leaving your horse on a high note and wanting more. Then place a large handful of food on the ground to counteract the negative punishment caused by ending the session. This also acts as an end of session signal and gives you time to remove your bum bag or other discriminative stimulus.

2. The rules of the game

When a horse exhibits an unwanted behaviour such as sniffing our pockets for treats we often label him as "naughty", "disrespectful" or "impolite". However, it is important to consider that politeness is a human concept that can vary depending from a culture to another. For example, in Russia turning down an alcoholic drink that is being offered is terribly offensive when in other countries such as the United Kingdom, it is not.

Unwanted behaviours such as sniffing pockets can be the result of the animal's ethogram – his repertoire of natural behaviours. For example, dogs sniff each other's butts when greeting so they can collect chemical information about their new friends. Of course, just like not sniffing your dog's butt doesn't make you an impolite person, a horse sniffing your pockets is not being disrespectful; he is just performing a natural explorative behaviour that is part of his ethogram.

Furthermore, unwanted behaviours may occur because they have been reinforced in the past. For example, if a horse has been given treats for sniffing a person he is obviously more likely to do it again. The horse is not being "naughty", he is being smart by simply repeating the behaviour that has earned him food in the past.

The following exercise will focus on teaching the horse to stand still and relaxed with his head forward; the opposite of searching, nibbling or pushing the trainer for treats. I decided to call this exercise "the rules of the game" because the way we tend to label horses as "disrespectful" is similar to inviting a friend over to play a game without explaining the rules and then calling him a cheat when he inevitably starts playing incorrectly. This exercise is the equivalent of explaining the rules to the player before starting the game.

To teach this exercise to your horse, you will need a clicker or voice bridge signal and protective contact to remain safe while the horse is learning the rules of the game. Protective contact assures safety for both the handler and horse; the handler can safely move away if the horse attempts to bite or push him and will not have to resort to the use of positive punishment to stay safe.

An example of bad (left photo) and better (right photo) food delivery. On the left, I am feeding Héros close to my body without extending my arm towards him. He is the one coming to me to get the food rather than me going to him.

TRAINING STEPS

Step 1: Start the exercise behind protective contact. This means a fence, gate or door should be between the horse and you. Place yourself by the side of the horse and simply wait for the horse to stand with his head forward rather than towards you. The horse should never be corrected for sniffing or nibbling the bum bag, if you feel unsafe simply step a little further away but never punish the horse. Simply wait for the horse to offer the desired behaviour; standing with his head forward.

Step 2: As soon as the horse moves his head away from your body, use your clicker to mark the exact moment when the horse offers the desired behaviour. Deliver the food quickly and away from your body. Ideally, the horse should be taking the treat with his head and body aligned and the food should be placed right underneath his chin to promote good posture.

Step 3: Repeat the process for no more than 5 minutes at first and end on a positive note (even if this means you only spend a couple of minutes on this exercise). Keep an eye on the horse's body language during the exercise; not only do you want to reinforce the horse for facing forward but you also want to encourage relaxation. Avoid reinforcing a horse who keeps his head away from your bum bag but pinches his nostrils and flattens his ears; this is not a relaxed horse who is ready to move to more complex exercises.

Héros standing still while I stand near his hindquarters.

Step 4: Once the horse has learned that standing forward and calm is crucial in winning the game, you can increase the difficulty by introducing movement and removing protective contact. Because you possess a desirable stimulus it is tempting for the horse to want to follow you, however, it is crucial for tasks such as picking up hooves and grooming that the horse learns to stand still while you move around his body.

Shaping the behaviour is crucial here; start by taking a small step backwards, click immediately while the horse is standing still and move back towards him to deliver the reinforcer. Repeat this step a few times before increasing the criteria, for example, move back two steps then click and treat.

THE RULES OF THE GAME WITH SCRATCHES

If you want to train a horse with a combination of both food and scratches you need to teach the rules of the game for both reinforcers. Just as a horse that hasn't been taught the rules may try to earn food by nudging you, a horse that hasn't been taught the rules when it comes to earning scratches may try to lean or swing his body into you in an attempt to get scratched.

For scratches, proceed exactly the same way as above; do not click or scratch a horse who is leaning into you, instead click and start scratching when the horse is standing still with all four feet on the floor. Protected contact is just as useful with scratches as with food; it will prevent the horse from accidently stepping on your feet in an attempt to get scratched.

TROUBLESHOOTING

What should I do if my horse does not appear relaxed during the exercise?

If your horse displays signs of tension, annoyance or over-arousal the first step is to re-evaluate the situation. Are you training in a calm and relaxed environment? Are there stimuli in the environment that could cause annoyance, fear and stress such as other horses, flies, bad weather, people or objects that the horse is afraid of? Is the horse hungry? Have you fed the horse before the training? Is your chosen reinforcer suitable for the horse or too highly valued? Are you feeding enough of the chosen reinforcer for the horse to gain satisfaction while chewing it? Does the horse have access to the chosen reinforcer outside the training session? Are other sources of food available during the training session such as a haynet? Does your rate of reinforcement cause frustration to your horse? These are a few of the many questions you should ask yourself when faced with such a problem.

Once you have taken care of any undesirable antecedent that may cause your horse to feel tense it is time to look at the timing of your bridge signal. Chances are you have been reinforcing the desired behaviour (facing forward) while the horse was displaying these signs of tension and they have become part of the behaviour. To change this, look for any behavioural sign of relaxation from your horse during the exercise then click and deliver the food reward as soon as you see an improvement. If you start with a horse displaying a tight mouth and a pronounced chin be ready to click when the mouth softens, if the ears are pinned look for any forward movement of the ears, if the horse is pawing in frustration click when all four feet are on the floor etc. Start by reinforcing any small, positive developments and you should eventually see improvement as long as you have addressed potential issues such as hunger, unsuitable environment, inappropriate reinforcers, rate of reinforcement etc.

If you are stuck do not hesitate to film the training session, not only so you can ask a more experienced trainer to review the footage, but also because you may be able to see a mistake that you couldn't spot during the actual session.

What should I do if my horse alternates between mugging me and standing forward?

Chances are you have accidentally created a behaviour chain where you end up with the horse putting his nose in the bum bag, then putting his head straight and putting his nose back in the bum bag again (or similar). This can occur if you click and treat the horse when in the desired position and then wait for him to move his head back toward you and away again before clicking and treating.

To avoid this problem, you need to stop and wait for the horse to put his head back straight before clicking and treating again. Use a higher rate of reinforcement by rewarding your horse a lot more when he is in the desired position. Wait for your horse to put his head in the desired position then click and treat. While he is chewing, he will keep his head in the desired position. Take advantage of this; click and treat. You may feel like a food distributor at first but you will quickly be able to space out the number of clicks and solve the problem.

What should I do if my horse moves back during step 4 of the exercise?

For step 4, the suggested shaping steps are: step back once, reinforce this a few times, and then raise the criteria by stepping two steps back. However, horses are all individual and your horse may need even smaller steps. For example, you may have to start by simply leaning back or moving a single foot.

It is also important to move quickly: move a step back, click, move back towards the horse and deliver the food as quickly as possible. If you are taking too much time doing all of this, you are adding a layer of difficulty by adding extra duration to the behaviour.

Moving back toward the horse after clicking is also very important, otherwise the horse will have to step back to take his reward from you.

3. Nose targeting

Nose targeting is an extremely useful skill to learn. It can be used to lead the horse in various situations such as trailer loading and is a building block to several behaviours such as backing up and leading.

For this exercise, you will need a clicker or voice bridge to precisely mark the desired behaviour and protective contact when first introducing the task.

TRAINING STEPS

Step 1: Place yourself by the side of your horse and present the target with your arm extended away from your body and towards the horse's nose. Make sure to present the target slowly and not suddenly move the target towards the horse's face or you may scare him. Generally, it is best to present the target a few centimetres away from the horse's nose as it is easier for him to touch, however, some horses may be scared and require the target to be placed further away.

Step 2: Wait until the horse touches it. Horses are naturally curious animals who investigate novel objects with their nose and whiskers so getting the first touch should be easy.

Step 3: Click and remove the target (you can place it behind your back or to your side) before delivering the food under the horse's nose and away from your body. If the horse does not touch the target you can simply click and reinforce him for extending his nose towards it.

Step 4: Repeat the process several times and on both sides. Keep in mind that because the target is associated with food, it has become a secondary reinforcer and therefore the presentation of the target is reinforcing whatever behaviour the horse was doing immediately before. Do not present the target if the animal is exhibiting unwanted behaviours such as mugging, leaning against the barrier or pawing. Be consistent by applying the same rules you taught the horse in the rules of the game exercise.

Step 5: Once the horse has learned to nose target and remains calm during the exercise, protective contact can be removed and the nose targeting skill can be generalised to other targets such as the trainer's hand or a ball.

Very enthusiastic horses like Spirit can be overwhelming to work
with when first getting started so use protective contact to build your
confidence and skills.

TROUBLESHOOTING

What should I do if my horse does not interact with the target?

If your horse <u>does not show any</u> explorative behaviours towards the novel object it is likely that he is suppressed due to past harsh training. It is not rare for horses to be punished for explorative behaviours such as moving their head to the side during a ride, attempting to eat leaves or sniffing the defecation of another horse. All these punishments can cause the horse to no longer offer behaviours in the presence of his trainer.

To solve the problem the horse needs to learn that explorative behaviours do pay off and do not result in positive punishment. Turn out your horse in a paddock with interesting objects for him to explore and click and treat any explorative behaviour. You can also set up food puzzles such as hiding pieces of food in a box filled with hay and objects.

It is also possible that the horse may be fearful of the object itself, to check if this is the case try changing the object you are using as a target.

What should I do if my horse bites the target rather than touching it?

Horses may bite the target if they have been accidently reinforced by doing so or if the trainer's timing is wrong (clicking too late). If your horse bites the target instead of touching it, try clicking earlier just when he is approaching his nose towards the target. After a few early clicks the horse will approach the target more carefully and you can progressively go back to clicking the complete behaviour.

Chapter 4
Basic handling and healthcare training

This chapter contains step-by-step instructions on training horses to willingly participate in some basic handling and healthcare procedures. Depending on the horse you own, you may not find all the training plans in this chapter useful; many plans such as touch and headcollar acceptance are designed to help the reader start young horses or retrain rescue animals. However, no matter what your goals with your horse are, reading these plans will definitely teach you how to improve your behaviour-shaping skills.

1. Touch acceptance

Touch acceptance is an essential skill for all horses to learn because it is the foundation of many behaviours such as accepting grooming and tack. Horses with good touch acceptance are also good candidates for the use of scratches as rewards and the use of stroking to soothe them during threatening events.

Typically, horses learn to accept touch at an early age when they are relatively fearless and still with their mother, but many develop aversion to being touched in certain areas of their bodies due to aversive experiences such as painful/threatening health care procedures or harsh handling.

Tips before you get started:

- Keep track of your horse's progress by rating his touch acceptance from 0 to 5 for each part of his body.

- First, teach the horse to stand still and be relaxed while you stand next to him by teaching him "the rules of the game" exercise that is part of the foundation training.

- Always start working on touch acceptance on an area that horses frequently mutual groom such as the neck and shoulder.

- Work at liberty to allow the horse to move away. Be careful not to corner the horse and make sure he has plenty of escape routes so that if he feels threatened he does not have to go through you to escape. With horses being prone to fight rather than flight, start by working behind protected contact to keep yourself safe. Placing yourself in protective contact may also help the horse feel less threatened and more comfortable.

TRAINING STEPS

Step 1: During this exercise, we break down touch into small components, making sure the horse is comfortable with each of the steps that lead him to be touched. Because touch typically starts by the human raising their arm/hand, this is where you will start.

While standing close to the body part you are working on, raise your arm slightly in front of you, click the horse for standing still and relaxed, lower your arm and reward. Repeat several times, progressively making bigger movements.

Step 2: Raise your arm slightly, this time in the direction of the horse's body, click the horse for standing still and relaxed, lower your arm and reward. Just as with step 1, repeat several times, progressively making bigger movements.

Step 3: Build up duration, raise your arm, hold it up for a couple of seconds, click, lower your arm and reward. Repeat a few times and progressively increase the duration.

Step 4: Raise your arm, place your hand a couple of centimetres away from the horse's skin, click, remove your hand and reward. Repeat several times until the horse is completely comfortable.

Lyviera and I illustrating step 4 of the touch acceptance training plan.

Step 5: Touch the horse's skin briefly, click, remove your hand and reward. Make sure to touch the horse confidently and not to tickle him by brushing him with the tip of your fingers. Repeat several times before moving on to step 6.

Step 6: Introduce your horse to the idea of being stroked by raising your arm and doing a short stroking motion in the air, a few centimetres away from his skin. Click mid stroke, remove your hand and reward. Repeat until the horse is completely comfortable.

Step 7: Touch the horse's skin and make a short stroking motion, click, remove your hand and reward. Repeat several times before introducing the horse to longer strokes.

Step 8: As the horse becomes more and more relaxed, progressively increase the duration of the strokes and introduce him to scratches. Do not forget to repeat the process on both sides and all over the horse body.

2. Teaching your horse to accept grooming

Once your horse has learned to accept and enjoy being touched you can introduce him to being touched by other items such as brushes.

TRAINING STEPS

Step 1: For any procedure that involves putting the horse in contact with a novel object always ensure the horse has good touch acceptance to start with.

Doing touch acceptance first may sound like a waste of time but
it is key in reducing the horse stress, boosting your chances
of success and preventing trigger stacking from occurring.

Step 2: Start the session by allowing the horse to inspect the grooming tools. You can encourage explorative behaviour by clicking and treating the horse for sniffing, touching the material etc.

Step 3: Take one of the brushes and approach your horse's neck or shoulder – do not touch the horse with the brush – click when the brush approaches the horse's body, remove the brush and reward your horse. Repeat several times. Start this exercise at the necessary distance: some horses may not even require this step while other horses may not allow the brush to be closer than a metre away from their skin. Pay attention to your horse's body language to know where you should start and progressively decrease the distance between the brush and the horse.

Step 4: Bring the brush towards the horse's skin but do not touch him with it, mimic a brushing/stroking motion while holding the brush, bridge, remove the brush and reward the horse. Start with short stroking motion only.

To encourage the horse to stand still during the process, no matter where you are standing, it is recommended that you start by teaching him the rules of the game exercise or at the very least always move back toward the horse's head to deliver food rewards.

Step 5: Repeat step 4 but this time doing longer brushing motion above the horse's skin.

Step 6: Briefly make contact with the horse's skin, click and immediately remove the brush before delivering the reward.

Step 7: Repeat step 6, this time leaving the brush on the horse for a longer period of time.

Step 8: Combine steps 4 and 7. Do a short brush stroke, click, remove the brush and reward your horse.

Step 9: Combine step 5 and 7. Do a longer brush stroke, click while brushing, remove the brush and reward your horse.

Step 10: From this step build up the number of strokes and progressively fade out the use of rewards. Work on this exercise by sections; a horse may easily accept grooming in neck/shoulder area but be uncomfortable in other areas of his body. For this reason, do not assume that because you successfully taught your horse to accept grooming at the neck area that he will be comfortable with you brushing his legs.

3. Teaching your horse to give his hooves

Teaching your horse to willingly give his hooves and remain calm during trimming and shoeing procedures is essential if you want to reduce the risk of an accident occurring to your farrier and reduce your animal's stress.

The following training plan is suitable for both horses that have never had their hooves handled before and horses that have had their hooves handled but are unreliable and difficult to handle.

TRAINING STEPS

Step 1: Before you even think of going near a hoof, the first and most important step is to teach your horse to willingly and calmly stand still. To do this, first teach the "rules of the game" to your horse. Place yourself by the side of your horse and wait for him to have his 4 feet on the floor with his head facing forward before using your bridge signal and delivering a reward. Repeat this step several times before adding a new layer of difficulty; take a step back, quickly bridge while your horse is standing still, move back toward your horse's head and give him the reward.

Step 2: Build up the number of steps you make until you are able to move all around the horse. If the horse moves at any point through this training, break it down into even smaller steps.

Step 3: Once you have got a pretty solid stand still behaviour, you can then progress to teaching touch acceptance for the legs. Start at the top of the shoulder and progressively travel down the horse legs, bridge while your hand is on the horse's leg and then move back toward the horse's head to reward him.

Break this behaviour down into small steps; do not just try to travel all the way from top to bottom in one go. There are no strict rules on when to bridge and reward because it will vary from one horse to the next but keep an eye on your horse at all times as he will tell you. If the horse is displaying signs of stress, annoyance or moving away, you have asked too much in one go. Always bridge and reward while the horse is calm and still.

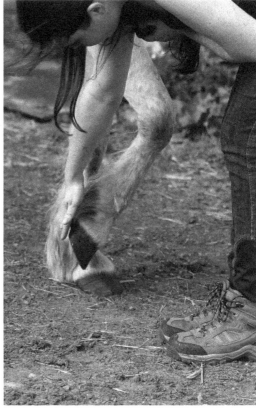

Spirit and I illustrating hoof targeting, an alternative to applying aversive pressure to the limb.

Step 4: Now that the horse is happy having a human move around his body and being touched all over his legs, you can start teaching him to give his hooves. Typically, this is done using negative reinforcement; an aversive is applied on the leg until the horse picks it up. While this of course can work, many horses will try to avoid the aversive in the first place by refusing to stand still or not let the person near their legs. In humane, science-based horse training we use the targeting technique instead.

Place your hand a few millimetres away from the horse's cannon and wait for the horse to move his leg, as soon as the skin comes into contact with your hand, bridge, remove your hand and quickly deliver the reward. At first, contact will be made accidentally but with repetitions the horse will learn that the criteria for reinforcement is to make contact with your hand using his leg.

Step 5: After some repetitions your horse should have understood that he must bend his leg to touch your hand. At this stage, you can start to progressively increase the distance between his cannon and your hand, this will cause your horse to have to lift his leg higher, making it more convenient for hoof care.

Step 6: The next criterion to work on is duration. The aim of this step is to introduce the horse to the idea of having to hold his leg in the air for a longer period of time and in future steps, these few additional seconds will provide you with enough time to position your hand underneath the hoof to provide support.

Adding duration is done very progressively by slightly delaying the bridge signal. Until now, you have been bridging at the exact moment when your horse's leg comes into contact with your hand so to start building duration simply count "1" in your head and then bridge. This will delay the bridge signal for about 0.5 seconds which should be a short enough time for the horse to still be making contact with your hand and a long enough time to start introducing him to the idea of duration.

Repeat this a few times, paying close attention to the horse's reaction to this change before adding a bit more duration to the behaviour, this time counting "1, 2" before bridging and rewarding.

Step 7: Of course, during hoof care the horse does not hold his hoof in the air, instead the farrier supports it. To introduce this idea to your horse, ask him to target your hand and while he is holding his leg up, slide your hand underneath his hoof and bridge immediately before letting go and rewarding.

The horse should get used to the idea quite quickly as long as you worked carefully on touch acceptance in step 3. You can then build up duration in a similar way to step 6. Try having a horse that allows you to support his leg for at 30 seconds before moving on to the next step.

Remember that the idea here is to provide support to the horse, not to restrain him. If the horse wants to put his hoof down do not try to hold on to it as you will cause him to become anxious and fearful instead of willing and happy. If anything, allowing him to take his hoof away will reassure him that there is nothing to fear about this situation. Next time just try to bridge before the horse feels the need to take his hoof away from your hand

Step 8: The farrier will use a variety of tools and put the horse legs in various position to shoe and trim, so do not forget to get your horse used to having his legs moved about and the sole being tapped (use the back of a hoof pick to imitate the banging of a hammer). As always, do things progressively and reward.

Step 9: Generalise the behaviour. Chances are, you won't be the one shoeing and trimming your horse and therefore it is essential for your horse to generalise his learning to other people. Ask a friend or family member to come up to the yard and do some training with you. Remember to decrease the criteria for reinforcement a little at first and do not hesitate to have your assistant work briefly on all the steps covered in the training plans before actually holding the hooves.

Beware that if your horse had previously bad experiences with the farrier, it may overshadow his training and therefore you may either have to pay your farrier to come for an hour to do some training with you and your horse or change farriers.

TROUBLESHOOTING

My horse won't lift his leg to target my hand.

Place your hand a few millimetres away from his skin, wait about 10 seconds giving the horse a chance of doing it on his own first, then touch the horse's cannon and use your bridge signal while touching, remove your hand and reward. After a few trials the horse should try to bend his leg to touch your hand and you can bridge and reward him for it.

If after trying this technique several times you have no sign of progress, you can ask a person to get the horse to step one step forward. This can be done using a nose target if the horse hasn't yet learned to lead calmly. Before your assistant asks your horse to move, place your hand in the right position, when the horse will step forward he will come into contact with your hand, bridge immediately and as accurately as possible and reward quickly. After a few trials your horse should get the idea and you won't need the assistance of a second person.

4. Teaching your horse to put his headcollar on

TRAINING STEPS

Step 1: Before you train your horse to accept a headcollar or a bridle it is best to work on touch acceptance first (see touch acceptance training plan); if your horse does not allow you to stroke his head, it will be a lot more challenging to teach him to accept a headcollar + your hands, than your hands alone.

Step 2: Place your hands on either side of the nose part of the headcollar and present it to your horse. Present the headcollar at a suitable distance; meaning far away enough not to cause the horse to want to flee but close enough for the horse to show interest in the item.

Step 3: Click and reinforce explorative behaviours such as sniffing and touching. Some horses may be more cautious than others and may simply stretch their neck towards the item but still maintain distance; work with whatever the horse offers and progress from there.

Step 4: After a few click and treats the horse will become more confident and investigate the headcollar more boldly. This is where you can start to be more selective on what earns a click and a treat and what doesn't. Your aim is to get the horse to slip his nose inside the noseband part so you must reinforce any little step that goes toward this goal behaviour.

If you are struggling shaping this behaviour you can try feeding through the hole of the noseband a few times. However, be aware that this technique may only be suitable for naïve horses; rescue horses may become conflicted between their desire to gain access to the food and their fear of the headcollar.

Don't pull the headcollar through your horse's nose instead let him put it on himself. This is especially important for horses with traumatic pasts who had little to no say about what was done to them.
They will blossom from having some control and choice.

Step 5: Once the horse reliably places his nose in the noseband you can start to build duration. You will need to reach a point where the horse is willing to keep his nose in the noseband for at least 5 seconds so that later on in the training you have time to buckle the headcollar. Duration can be introduced by slightly delaying your click. So, for example, if until now you used to click 0.5 seconds into the behaviour, you will now try to click 1 second into the behaviour instead. After a few repetitions, you can increase the criteria for duration – now waiting 2 seconds before clicking and treating the horse. Keep increasing the duration progressively until you have a horse who not only puts his nose in the headcollar on his own but also stay in position until you click.

Step 6: When you are satisfied with your results you can start working on another aspect of headcollar acceptance: accepting the crown strap. For teaching this I found that attaching a long piece of twine to one of the crown strap holes is very useful.

There are a few ways to do this, you can either start working at the poll straight away (can be suitable for naïve horses) or start working at the base of the neck (may be more appropriate for rescue horses) and progressively make your way towards the poll.

While standing on the left of the horse, hold the twine (connected to the crown strap) in your right hand while holding the buckle strap in your left hand, pass the twine over the horse (in an appropriate position for the horse) and click the horse for standing still, let go of the twine and reward your horse. Do this a few times before progressing a step further.

The twine extends the size of the crown giving you the opportunity
to use as small steps as the horse required and to quickly get
the headcollar off if he gets threatened.

Step 7: Once the horse is comfortable with the twine/crown strap being passed over his neck or poll (depending on where you start) you can pass the twine inside the buckle and very slightly tighten. Because you are using a piece of twine you will be able to tighten less than you will have to if only using a crown strap, this allows you to make the process as progressive as required for your horse.

While sliding the twine into the buckle, click, then quickly slide the twine back out before delivering the treat. Repeat several times and progressively slide the twine further into the buckle as you go. Always keep an eye on your horse's body language during the process; it will let you know when the horse is ready to take it a step further or need you to slow down the process.

Step 8 (if starting at the base of the neck): Repeat step 6 and 7 but this time higher up the horse's neck.

Step 9: Once you've got these two behaviours sorted (putting nose in noseband + accepting the crown strap it is time to put them together. Start by presenting the noseband to the horse, wait for the horse to place his nose in it, then pass the twine over the horse and into the buckle. Click, remove the headcollar and quickly deliver the reward.

Do not attempt to tighten the crown strap on your first trial, after all this is the first time your horse will experience both elements of the headcollar at the same time. Buckle the headcollar in place over a few trials.

Step 10: For your horse to reliably accept the headcollar do not forget to practice regularly and in different settings. Make use of real-life rewards to maintain the behaviour (e.g. turnout) and avoid putting the headcollar on <u>only</u> for potentially aversive events (e.g. veterinarian visits), otherwise the horse will start to perceive the headcollar as an unpleasant stimulus and may start refusing to put it on.

5. Teaching your horse to walk on a lead

Leading should be taught at liberty first in a safe enclosed area and in protected contact if necessary. The lead should only be added later once the horse already knows how to perform the desired behaviour.

TRAINING STEPS

Step 1: To teach your horse to walk on a lead it is important to first teach him to nose target (see nose targeting training plan) so you can use the targeting technique to capture forward movement during this exercise.

Step 2: Preferably start the training at liberty in a safe enclosed area before adding the headcollar and lead. While standing slightly in front of your horse, present the target approximately a metre away from his nose.

Step 3: Wait for the horse to move towards the target, click to mark the forward movement and then quickly remove the target and deliver the reward. You do not have to wait for your horse to touch the target to click as you are only using the target as a tool to motivate forward movement.

Step 4: Repeat this step several times. When the horse no longer hesitates to move towards the target you can start to add some more movement: present the target, wait for the horse to move forward and start moving alongside him while holding the target, click the horse for following, remove the target and deliver the reward.

Be aware that some horses may become frustrated to see the target being moved away from them, especially if you made the mistake of clicking the horse for touching the target rather than for moving toward the target. In this case make sure to progress slowly, ask little, reinforce often and pay close attention to your horse's body language.

Step 5: Once your horse is happy to walk along while following the target you can start fading it out. Start by presenting the target, when the horse starts walking, start walking, remove the target while walking and quickly click and treat the horse for moving forward without the target in front of him. Repeat this process progressively asking your horse to make more and more steps without the target. Eventually the target will no longer be required.

Step 6: Now that your horse can follow you at liberty you can introduce the headcollar and the lead. Get the horse used to the process by revisiting all the previous steps but this time while wearing the headcollar. Do not forget to practice in different places and conditions in order to generalise the skill.

Step 7: If you wish, you can introduce your horse to a tactile cue (tension on the lead). This must be done very carefully and only near the end of the training in order for the tactile cue not to be perceived as an aversive by the horse.

Teaching a tactile cue to your horse is useful if you plan on having a conventional horse person handle your horse from time to time, as typically equestrians are taught to pull on the lead to prompt forward movement. A horse who has never experienced this may get confused but this doesn't necessary mean that you must put your horse through negative reinforcement based training, instead it means that you should teach him conventional cues using positive reinforcement.

Start by creating a small tension on the lead rope, wait a second then present the target, wait for the horse to make a step toward the target, click the forward movement and reward.

Before introducing the cue	Before introducing the cue
Target = forward movement	Tension on the lead = no response
While introducing the cue	**After learning**
Tension on the lead + target = forward movement	Tension on the lead = forward movement

When introducing the tactile cue, the tension should be small enough not to be aversive to your horse. This means the horse's behaviour shouldn't change; there should be no sign of stress in his body language and no attempt to get relief from the tension. The tension should start neutral and become a cue through its association with the target and the reward.

This process must be repeated numerous times for the horse to learn the new cue; eventually the horse will start offering forward movement following tension on the lead.

6. Teaching your horse to accept sprays

Whether you wish to apply fly spray in summer, detangle your horse's mane or use a first aid spray, having the collaboration of your horse makes the process easier and safer.

Spirit checking out the water I am spraying by his side.
He is looking more curious than threatened.

TRAINING STEPS

Step 1: For this exercise, it is advisable to fill an empty spray bottle with water. This way you won't waste your products and the horse can safely investigate the bottle with his mouth if desired and won't accidentally receive harmful chemicals in his eye when you are spraying the air.

Step 2: Present the bottle at a distance from your horse and encourage explorative behaviour by clicking and treating the horse for sniffing, touching etc. the bottle.

Step 3: Once the horse is comfortable with touching the bottle take a few steps back and extend your hand away to spray. Click and reward your horse for standing still.

How far from the horse you need to stand will depend on the individual's threshold of reactivity; ideally you should spray far away enough not to cause the animal to want to flee but close enough for him to still show interest.

Step 4: Alternate between spraying and asking the horse to touch the bottle. This will provide you with information regarding how fearful the horse is and whether or not the horse is ready for the next step; is the horse hesitating to touch the bottle or is he confident touching it?

Step 5: Bring the bottle towards a part of the horse's body (neck/shoulder area is a good place to start) without touching him; click and treat the horse for standing still.

Step 6: If the horse is comfortable with the bottle being near his body you can progress to touching him with the bottle. Click, remove the bottle and reward to reinforce your horse for standing still. Progressively increase the duration of the touch.

Step 7: Once the horse has successfully completed the previous steps you can start spraying close to his body. But just like with step 3 you must spray away first. Spray, click, remove the bottle and reward the horse for standing still.

Step 8: Progressively spray closer to the horse's body until you are able to spray directly on him. Repeat the same process for different parts of the body.

7. Teaching your horse to take wormer

Squirting some water into Spirit's mouth as part of the wormer training.

TRAINING STEPS

Step 1: Start by presenting an empty syringe to your horse. Click and treat explorative behaviours such as licking and sniffing. If your horse has had bad experiences with worming, he will be more hesitant and you will need to be more patient and possibly have to reward smaller steps such as looking at the syringe.

Step 2: Position the syringe towards the lips, click and reward your horse for touching it with his lips. At first, the horse may try to touch it with his nose so be sure to present the syringe in such a way that it is easy for him to touch it with his lips.

Step 3: Gently insert the syringe between the lips, click, remove the syringe and reward. Because of the teeth, it is generally easier to do this by the side of the mouth (at the junction of the lips) rather than by the front. However, horses can be taught to open their mouth for the syringe with a progressive approach and well timed clicks.

It is recommended to do the entire process at liberty and without taking hold of the animal's head, as restraint is likely to make the experience aversive.

Step 4: Progressively insert the syringe deeper inside the horse's mouth without forgetting to click and reward.

Step 5: Once the horse has learned to take the syringe in his mouth, put liquid inside it (water or apple juice). Insert the syringe just as before and squirt only a little bit of the liquid in, click immediately, remove the syringe and reward. The liquid will come as a surprise to the horse, so start by only squirting a little bit in before training him to take the entire syringe.

Step 6: Once the horse confidently takes the syringe and lets you empty its contents you can give him the real wormer. It is likely that the medication will not taste good to the horse so it is important to give him fake wormers (using water or apple juice) a few times a year so he does not systematically associate the syringe with bad tasting medicine.

8. Teaching your horse to load and travel in a trailer/horsebox

The following training plan is suitable for introducing a naïve horse to loading and travelling in a trailer or to reintroduce trailers to a horse who has become fearful of them. Keep in mind that some horses won't necessarily need to go through all the steps in the training plan while others may need you to add additional steps. The term 'trailer' is used in this training plan but the same plan applies to a horsebox.

To teach or reintroduce trailer loading you can use targeting, free shaping or a combination of the two. A horse that is very confident with nose targeting but is fearful of trailers may feel conflicted between his desire to reach the target and his fear of the trailer; therefore, free shaping may be better for him. But a naïve horse with little training experience may find free shaping difficult and frustrating and be more at ease with the use of a target.

TRAINING STEPS

Step 1: Introduce the trailer to your horse, walk all around it, allowing the horse to sniff and lick the trailer if he wishes, this is your horse collecting information about the novel object.

Make sure to remove partitions from the vehicles at the beginning of the training to maximise space and light. Place a haynet inside the trailer so the horse can eat when practicing duration in step 10.

Tal and Ronnie watching Ceri prepare the horsebox for training. For a herd animal like the horse, having a friend present during training sessions can help him feel safer. It also offers opportunity for social learning to occur and reduces the risk of trigger stacking linked with separation anxiety.

Step 2: Approach the bottom of the ramp. If your horse doesn't want to approach it use the target to motivate forward movement or free shape the small steps he makes towards the ramp. When the horse stretches his neck to inspect the ramp click and reward him for exploring the object. Do not proceed to the next step until the horse is happy to stand still and calm at the bottom of the ramp.

Step 3: Present the target in such a way that the horse must place one hoof on the ramp to touch it. As soon as your horse put his hoof on the ramp click and reward. It does not matter if he didn't touch the target, what matters is that he placed a hoof on the ramp.

Do not worry if the horse removes his hoof from the ramp after you clicked. This simply means that after a few repetitions you will have to build up the duration of how long he keeps his hoof on the ramp by slightly delaying the click.

Repeat several times before moving on to step 4.

Step 4: Present the target a little bit further away so the horse must place both front hooves on the ramp. Click and reward. Between each reward allow the horse to back off from the ramp. Repeat this step a few times before moving to the next step.

Step 5: Ask the horse to put both front feet on the ramp one more time, this time mark a small pause of 2 seconds before clicking and rewarding. Repeat the step progressively increasing the amount of time the horse must stand still on the ramp before being rewarded and backing off.

Step 6: Using the target, get your horse to place 3 hooves on the ramp, click immediately when the back leg touches the ramp and reward. Repeat several times.

Step 7: Repeat the same procedure but this time with all 4 feet on the ramp. After this step it is a good idea to work on standing still with 4 feet on the ramp. Exactly as done in step 5.

Step 8: Still using the target ask the horse to move further into the trailer, this time standing with his 4 feet on the ramp but his head inside the trailer. Click and reward for moving forward. Back up and repeat the procedure a few times before going back on working on standing still as in step 7 but this time with the head inside the trailer.

Step 9: Continue to move further inside the trailer in a progressive manner until all 4 feet are in the trailer.

Step 10: Once the horse can go all the way into the trailer he should be confident enough to follow you in the trailer without the need for a target to be presented. Keep the target close by in case there is any hesitation.

<u>Work on duration by:</u>

- Walking in the trailer, pausing for 5 seconds, clicking, rewarding and walking back out.
- Walking in the trailer, pausing for 10 seconds, clicking, rewarding and walking back out.
- Walking in the trailer, pausing for 20 seconds, clicking, rewarding and walking back out.
- Keep increasing the duration until the horse is happy to stand inside the trailer for minutes at a time.

Step 11: Add the partitions, front bar and back chain (if using a trailer rather than a horsebox) progressively. Do not forget that because you are adding new things that the horse hasn't experienced before, you will need to reduce the amount of time you are expecting him to stand in the trailer. At first, simply load and unload immediately before adding standing time.

Step 12: Practice loading, tying the horse up and leaving the horse alone in the trailer for a few seconds before clicking and reappearing to reward him. Very progressively increase the duration of time the horse has to stay on his own in the trailer with the ramp(s) down.

Step 13: Ask a second person to assist you and lift the ramp back up slightly (about 10% up). Click your horse for standing still and reward while the second person puts the ramp back down. Repeat several times, progressively increasingly how far up the ramp gets lifted.

Depending on the transport you are using you may also have to practice lifting up the front ramp.

Step 14: Practice step 12 again but this time with the ramp(s) up.

Step 15: Run the engine while the horse is next to the vehicle before moving to the next step. It is important to determine if the horse is afraid of the sound of the engine before practicing running the engine with the horse in the trailer. If the horse is afraid, use targeting and treats to create a positive association with the sound of the engine.

Do not force the horse to stand directly by the vehicle if he is afraid, instead start at a distance with which he is comfortable and progressively reduce the distance between him and the vehicle.

Step 16: Load the horse and ask a second person to run the vehicle for less than a minute. Stay with the horse for his first time. If the horse is completely comfortable you can leave him on his own on the second trial.

Step 17: Repeat the procedure by leaving the horse in the box with the engine running for a few minutes. Reward your horse before unloading him.

Step 18: Load and drive the horse slowly and on a straight line for no longer than 30 seconds, click, reward your horse and unload. Increase the duration of the drive progressively and start taking turns slowly; you will know when you can increase the duration because the horse should not hesitate to load.

Step 19: For maximum reliability, practice loading in different areas and in different weather conditions.

TROUBLESHOOTING

I do not own my own trailer or only have limited access to one.

If you do not have a trailer/horsebox at your disposal there are still exercises that you can do that somewhat simulate trailer loading. For example, to simulate walking on the ramp try teaching your horse to walk over a tarpaulin or other novel/noisy surface available to you. To simulate walking through the partitions and standing in the middle, make a small corridor using poles and jumping wings. To simulate the obscurity of the trailer, teach your horse to walk and stand in a stable or stall. Combine all the above into one exercise to increase complexity.

Chapter 5
Fitness related behaviours

In this chapter, you will find step-by-step tutorials to develop behaviours such as stretching and lunging that promote body awareness, flexibility and athleticism. Traditionally, the movements explained in this chapter are trained through the use of negative reinforcement and positive punishment, which causes a certain amount of fear to the animal and cause him to adopt an unhealthy posture when getting started with the exercise. For example, naïve horses who are taught to back up through swinging of the rope will initially back up while holding their head high and their back hollow. With the use of positive reinforcement, the naïve horse is more relaxed and more focused on the exercise than on escaping the aversive; this causes him to start with a healthier posture.

1. Teaching your horse to back up

Backing up on cue is an important skill for a horse to learn; not only does it make everyday handling easier but it is also a good fitness exercise that causes the back to lift and flex and stimulates the sacroiliac area. It is a useful preliminary exercise to collection as it strengthens the muscles involved in engagement.

With the technique provided below you will easily achieve long, marching backward steps with a horse who naturally keeps his head and neck low without the use of restriction.

Lyviera backing up through the use of targeting.

TRAINING STEPS

Step 1: Place yourself by the side of the horse and ask him to touch the target with his nose a couple of times. This way the horse is already focused on the target before you introduce the new behaviour.

Step 2: Present the target in front of the horse's nose but this time do not click and treat if the horse touches it. Instead, use it to lure the horse's nose towards his chest; because of the position of the target the horse is likely to take a step back to touch it.

Step 3: Mark the precise moment when the horse takes a step back, remove the target and quickly deliver the reward. The horse does not necessarily have to touch the target with his nose to earn a click and treat, what you are rewarding here is the step back. The target is only used as a tool to get the behaviour.

Step 4: Repeat the process a few times, initially only requiring the horse to take a single step back to gain reinforcement. Once the horse has completed the desired behaviour successfully a few times in a row you can raise your criteria, requiring the horse to make 2 steps rather than 1 to earn reinforcement. Once the horse achieves this a few times, increase the criteria once again by only reinforcing the horse for making more than 2 steps. A good goal to work towards is for your horse to be capable of making a total of 10 steps and maintaining rhythm throughout.

Step 5: Depending on the goals you have for your horse, you will need to generalise his knowledge of the back up to other environments such as the trail; to other people such as the groom; and to other situations such as under saddle or while lunging.

TROUBLESHOOTING

What if my horse does not back up?

Health problems may cause a horse to have difficulties backing up so first consult your veterinarian; if they give your horse a clean bill of health proceed with the following:

If your horse does not back up when the target is placed between his nose and chest, look for other behaviours that go in the direction of your goal behaviours such as a weight shift or a lift of the leg.

If the horse seems really interested in the target but is only touching it and not backing up try to be patient and wait for a while; if the nose targeting behaviour doesn't lead to reinforcement the horse is likely to try something else, such as backing up. Be aware that some horses may get frustrated; therefore, it is essential to look at the horse's body language and reinforce whatever small steps they make toward the goal behaviour.

If, after trying out these ideas, you are still not getting any results try to set up the environment so the horse will have to back up at some point and be ready to click and treat when he does. For example, put poles to each side of the horse and in front of him so if he wants to move the only option available involves backing out. Of course, only use this solution if the horse is completely comfortable with poles and fencing; do not use temporary electric fencing tape that may be associated with aversive experiences (receiving an electric shock) or the horse will be nervous.

2. Teaching your horse to move his hips and shoulders

The following training plans can be used to teach your horse to move his hips and shoulders both towards and away from you. Not only is this skill convenient for everyday handling but it is also a fantastic fitness exercise that promotes suppleness and body awareness.

Sequence showing Lyviera moving her shoulders towards me. (1) The cue is given (my flat hand facing her shoulder); (2) She moves her shoulders in direction to the target; (3) She receives a click when her shoulder makes contact with my hand.

Lyviera starting to move her hip towards the target.

TRAINING STEPS (toward the handler)

Step 1: Start by positioning the target a few millimetres away from the animal's skin. Your position may vary according to what body part you want your animal to target and what targeting equipment you are using. For example, for shoulder targeting you can face the shoulder while holding a small target. For the hips, it is recommended to use a target stick so you can maintain a safe distance between you and your horse's hips.

Step 2: Because the target is held so close to his skin the horse will accidently come into contact with it when he fidgets. When this occurs immediately click, remove the target and reward.

Step 3: Repeat step 2 several times before increasing the distance between your horse's skin and the target; the horse will have to do a bigger movement in order to come in contact with the target and earn reinforcement.

Step 4: Work on both sides. Horses are naturally asymmetric and you will find that just because your horse successfully shoulder targets on the right, it will not necessarily follow that he can successfully target on the left. Be patient and work more progressively on his weaker side.

TRAINING STEPS (away from the handler)

Step 1: Once the horse has learned to move his hips or shoulders towards you when cued to do so with the target you can teach him to move his body the opposite way; away from you. To teach this you will need to pass the target stick over the horse's body and reach toward the opposite shoulder/hip. This can be tricky because horses with a past of aversive based training can react nervously at a stick being passed over their back. If this is the case with your horse, your first goal is to desensitise the horse to having the target passed over him. Do this by breaking down the movement into small parts and feeding your horse during the process; this will associate the movement of the target stick going over his back with something pleasurable. Once the horse no longer shows signs of fear with having the stick being passed over his back you can start teaching shoulder/hip away.

Step 2: Just as with shoulder/hip toward, place the target a few millimetres away from the skin and wait for the horse to bump into the target; click, remove the target and quickly reward.

Step 3: Repeat the process several times before moving the target further away from the skin.

TROUBLESHOOTING

My horse does not make contact with the target, what should I do?

First, it is best to only start doing this exercise once the horse has gained some training experience. Training based on the use of positive reinforcement is quite different to conventional training as it requires the horse to actively search for potential solutions rather than reacting to aversive stimuli. A horse who didn't go through the foundation exercises will struggle with such a complex task because he does not know that he has to search for a solution to the problem.

However, even horses with some experience with positive reinforcement training may struggle and need assistance. In this case, you can make contact yourself by touching the animal with the target, then click, remove the target and reward. It is important not to systematically touch the animal with the target on each repetition, always allow some time (about 10 seconds) for the horse to give it a try first. After a few repetitions, you will find your animal seeking the target by himself.

My horse reacts fearfully to the target being placed near his body.

The target should be perceived as a pleasurable stimulus because it provides the horse with the opportunity to earn rewards. If this is not the case, go back to nose targeting and also work on desensitising the horse to having the target around his body. Horses with a past of aversive-training may react fearfully to the target being near their body as it reminds them of past training especially if the target resembles a whip. If you are struggling with changing your horse's emotional response to the target and its placement, you can also use a different target; frisbees, cones and even your own hand can make good targets.

My horse turns around and tries to touch the target with his nose instead of his body.

It is important to make sure you have taught your horse to stand by teaching the rules of the game exercise; this will make the animal less likely to turn around and touch the target with his nose. It can also be useful to change the target you are using. So, for example, if you usually use a cone for nose targeting change to using a stick with a tennis ball on the end of it.

Finally, if your horse insists on touching the target with his nose, do more than just not reinforcing the behaviour; try to show him what the desired response is by using the technique explained in the "my horse does not make contact with the target" troubleshooting question.

Now that I have taught my horse to do this, he constantly swings his hips/shoulders towards me without being cued to do so.

This often occurs when the trainer chooses to use his hand as a target rather than a target stick or other item (such as a cone). To use his hand, the handler must be quite close to the horse's body and the horse can accidently learn to associate the handler's position with the exercise. Using the position of a target as a cue makes it easier for the horse to determine when to offer the exercise and when not to.

However, it is still possible to use your hand as a target but you must make it clear to the horse that it's your hand position rather than your body position that dictates when he should move and when he shouldn't. A good exercise to practice this is to randomly alternate between asking the horse to move his shoulder/hip and other exercises such as standing still and forward. It is, of course, essential for the trainer to only reinforce the horse for moving his shoulder/hip when cued to do so and ignore the times where he does it without being cued.

3. Teaching your horse to flex at the poll

Teaching your horse to flex his poll will stimulate the joints and muscles at the top of his neck and poll and prepare him (alongside teaching him to back up) to work on collection.

TRAINING STEPS

Step 1: Starting to teach poll flexion is easy, the challenge mostly lies in the last few steps involving putting the behaviour on cue and building up duration. Place yourself by the side of your horse and using a target, lure your horse's nose onto the vertical by placing the target under the horse's chin.

Step 2: Click when the horse achieves the desired position (head on the vertical or just in front of the vertical), remove the target and deliver the reward.

Step 3: As long as the horse has previously learned to nose target during foundation training you should easily get the desired behaviours within a few repetitions. Introduce the idea of duration by slightly delaying the click. So, for example, if you used to click 1 second into the poll flexion, try to click 2 seconds instead and progressively increase the duration until the horse can maintain poll flexion for at least 5 seconds.

Héros before (left) and after (right) poll flexion cue

Step 4: Work on establishing a new cue that does not involve the use of the target. This is important so the horse can learn to flex his poll without assistance and can do so no matter where you are standing. I personally use the same cue to request poll flexion and collection as they will become one as you eventually advance in your training.

Start by giving your new cue this can be whatever you want; for me it's a hand movement above the wither, wait a second and then present the target. When the horse flexes his poll, click, remove the target and reward. Repeat this several times (and over several sessions) until the horse starts offering poll flexion without the use of the target.

Before learning the new cue	Before learning the new cue
Position of the target = poll flexion	Your new cue = no response
While learning the new cue	**After learning the new cue**
Your new cue + target = poll flexion	Your new cue = poll flexion

Step 5: Once you've taught your new cue you will have to start working on duration once more but this time without the target. You will find that your horse will struggle significantly more to maintain a correct poll flexion without the assistance of the target as he can no longer use it as a point of reference. This means you will have to pay close attention to the timing of your click; a wrongly timed click can quickly teach a horse to overflex. After a few sessions and consistent reinforcement, the horse will become more confident with how to position his head.

4. Teaching your horse to walk over raised poles

This exercise has similar benefits to backing up; it strengthens the muscles involved in engagement and stimulates the sacroiliac area. It also requires the horse to lift and flex from the shoulder and elbow, all the way through the back to the hip, stifle and hock.

TRAINING STEPS

Step 1: Place a pole on the ground and allow your horse to engage in explorative behaviour. You can encourage a shy horse to be more confident with his exploration by clicking and rewarding small exploration attempts such as looking at the pole or sniffing it at a distance. Once your horse is confident with the object (i.e. shows no sign of fear), move on to step 2.

Step 2: Using a target stick, lead your horse over a pole placed on the ground, click when the horse steps over it and reward once he is on the other side.

Step 3: Repeat a few times on both sides before progressively raising the height of the pole until it is around knee height. Encourage slow movement over the pole by walking slowly yourself. Precisely mark the moment where your horse flexes his hip, stifle and hock to clear the pole. Keep your horse's head and neck low by keeping the target stick low.

Step 4: Add a couple more poles (one at a time) to make the exercise more complex. Place the poles about 90 cm apart and adjust the distance between them if your horse struggles with keeping a smooth gait. As you add more poles, start to move away from a continuous schedule of reinforcement and towards a variable or fixed schedule of reinforcement. (See the "reinforce your horse" section)

Step 5: Work on fading out the target stick. A good way to do this is to use the target stick to lead the horse toward the pole, and then remove it as the horse starts walking over the pole. Reintroduce the target stick if the horse deviates from the trajectory and remove it once the horse is on the right track. Because you clicked for the wanted behaviour (walking over the pole) rather than for your horse to catch the target, fading it out shouldn't be too difficult.

AND WHAT ABOUT JUMPING?

Once you have taught your horse to walk over raised poles and to trot on cue you can introduce him to jumping small fences. Follow similar steps as for walking over raised poles but this time also cue your horse to trot after the target.

If your horse easily becomes frustrated when following moving targets, consider throwing your target instead. Stationary targets – a non-moving target to which the horse is sent to – are also suitable for pole work.

5. Teaching your horse to trot on cue

TRAINING STEPS

Step 1: Choose the right moment and environment to train the behaviour; your horse will need to be forward going but this shouldn't be as a result of external threats (for example, windy weather) or unpleasant emotions (for example, separation anxiety).

Step 2: One way to get your horse to trot is first to ask the horse to follow you (see teach your horse to walk on a lead), reinforce him for following you and then start running. Most horses will follow by picking up the trot.

Alternative ways to motivate trot are to use a target stick or teach the horse to play with a ball as during play, the horse is likely to pick up trot (and even canter) to chase after the ball.

Preferably teach your horse to trot while at liberty or on a loose lead and avoid creating tension on the lead.

Step 3: As soon as the horse starts trotting, click, stop and deliver the reward. Repeat several times before working on duration; this means you will stop clicking and rewarding immediately and instead ask the horse to make a few more strides before earning a click and a treat. Increase duration progressively. So, for example, start by asking for 2 to 3 strides a few times before moving on to asking for 5 to 6 strides. Of course, how you build up duration will depend on your horse; some horses need to start with a higher rate of reinforcement than others.

Héros trotting after the target stick.

Step 4: Now that your horse trots willingly for a few strides you can change the cue to something more practical such as a voice cue. This is done by first giving the cue of your choice, wait a second and then give your old cue. Depending upon how you obtained the trot this is either you running or the horse following an object. When the horse starts trotting, click immediately and reward. Repeat this several times until the horse starts to respond to your new cue alone. When you have accomplished this, you can add duration to the behaviour.

Before learning the new cue	Before learning the new cue
Handler running = horse trots	Your new cue = no response
While learning the new cue	**After learning the new cue**
Your new cue + running = trot	Your new cue = trot

Step 5: Work on generalising the cue. Start giving the trot cue in a variety of contexts such as during lunging or long lining and in a variety of places such as when out walking or in the arena. Keep in mind that during generalisation you will need to temporarily reduce your criteria of reinforcement. So, for example, if your

horse can trot comfortably for several minutes when out walking, do not expect him to straight away be able to trot for several minutes while lunging.

Héros trotting on verbal cue around some cones. I keep my target stick close in case I need to use my old cue (in my case a fast-moving target).

TROUBLESHOOTING

My horse gets over aroused during this exercise.

During "high-energy exercises" horses can become over aroused. Signs of over arousal may include snatching food out of hand, nipping, bucking etc. For safety reasons, it is important to keep your horse as calm as possible during these exercises.

First, it is important to only start exploring high-energy exercises once you have built a solid training foundation; your horse should be able to perform all the basic behaviours (take treats, stand, target and walk) calmly, confidently and with no sign of frustration.

If during a training session you feel the energy is starting to run a little bit too high (for example, the horse starts to take the treats less delicately than usual), take a break from the exercise and instead ask for simple, stationary behaviours such as targeting, lowering the head, picking up an item etc. Your horse should quickly calm down and you can soon restart the exercise.

I want to teach my horse to canter on cue.

To teach your horse to canter on cue, you can use a similar procedure. I found that during play, horses tend to pick up canter more easily than if you try to run and ask them to follow.

6. Teaching your horse to perform the Spanish walk

Héros targeting with his knee.

Spanish walk is a good exercise to improve co-ordination and body awareness but taught incorrectly has the potential to be dangerous. Therefore, I recommend only teaching it once both you and your horse have developed a solid understanding of humane, science-based training.

To teach this behaviour we use body targeting. Not only because it is an easy way to get the wanted behaviour and to control at what height the legs are lifted, but also because the target stick ensures that the behaviour is on cue from the start (so the horse is less likely to randomly hit you with his leg) and allows you to stay at a safe distance from the horse's legs.

TRAINING STEPS

Step 1: The first step is to teach your horse to touch a target with his knee. This is done in a similar way as when teaching hip or shoulder target. Place the target a few millimetres away from your horse's knee and wait for him to make contact with it.

Step 2: When the horse moves his leg and makes contact with the target, click immediately, remove the target and reward. It can very difficult for the horse to achieve this on his own, especially as at this point in his training he most likely has learned to nose target and back up following a target so he is likely to offer these two behaviours and get frustrated when they don't work.

In this situation, you have 2 possible solutions:

1. You can wait for a few seconds, then simultaneously touch the knee with the target and click, remove the target and reward. Repeat this process a few times,

always leaving some time before actually touching the horse with the target so he has a chance to make contact with the target himself.

2. You can present the target a few millimetres from the horse's knee, then cue the horse to move forward. When moving, the horse will make contact with the target and you can immediately click, remove the target and reward. After a few repetitions the horse will understand that he has to touch the target with his knee.

Step 3: Once the horse has successfully learned to lift his leg to touch the target you can progressively increase the distance between his knee and the target, this will encourage him to lift his leg higher.

Step 4: Practice on both legs.

Step 5: Introduce your horse to the idea of alternating which leg he has to lift by asking him to lift the right one, reward, then the left, reward and repeat.

Step 6: To start introducing forward movement to your horse, place the target further away from him. To reach the target he will not only have to raise his leg but also reach forward. To keep his balance, he will naturally move his back leg. You will need to work on both legs and repeat several times before asking for move steps.

Step 7: Start asking for more steps and move from a continuous schedule of reinforcement to a variable schedule of reinforcement (see the "reinforcing behaviours" section). As you progress and ask your horse to do more steps in a row, remember that you will get the best result by avoiding a fixed schedule of reinforcement and by reinforcing the best tries.

TROUBLESHOOTING

My horse gets confused between backing up following the target and knee targeting.

Your horse is most probably confused by how similar both cues look. A good way to teach these differences is to randomly alternate between cueing Spanish walk and back up. You can also change the cue altogether by removing the use of the target for one of the behaviours or adding something to it such as a voice cue.

7. Teaching your horse to perform circles

Teaching your horse to circle can help him to become more supple, improve his coordination and counteract natural asymmetry. One common problem with lunging and circling is that more often than not the horse "falls in" on the circle, meaning the centre of mass is shifted towards the inside front leg. While this issue is mostly due to natural asymmetry, it is made worse by the use of aversives; the horse looks to the outside of the circle, bending his head, neck and therefore spine the opposite way because he wants to get away from the aversive.

For a horse to correctly navigate a circle he needs to bend his spine in such a way that it is aligned with the circle, this affects the position of the pelvis and results in his inside hind leg stepping under the centre of mass. This is not possible with the head looking out! Of course, it is completely possible to teach a horse to bend properly using aversives but it is significantly harder to achieve than with positive reinforcement, especially for beginners.

Once the horse has understood the concept (walking outside the cones), the target stick can be faded out.

TRAINING STEPS

Step 1: You can teach your horse to circle no matter how little equipment you have. If you have a round pen available, you can use it with the horse walking outside the round pen and you inside the round pen. If you don't have a round pen available, you can use cones and tape or blocks and poles to create your circle. If you don't have this luxury then some markers (cones, buckets, whatever you find) can be enough.

Start by setting up your circle; create a 10m diameter circle using 4 to 8 markers.

Step 2: Using a target stick guide your horse onto the circle, click when he is passing on the outside of the first marker, remove the target and reward. Go around the circle a couple of times, bridging and rewarding your horse every time he passes a marker.

Don't forget to do this on both sides. Be aware that one side will require more work than the other due to natural asymmetry.

Step 3: Start fading the target stick. Present the target to motivate your horse to walk toward the next marker, when the horse is close to the marker, remove the target, click when the horse is passing the marker and reward. Repeat several times with all markers, progressively using the target stick less and less.

Step 4: Once the horse understands that he has to pass on the outside of each marker, you can move on from a continuous schedule of reinforcement and towards a variable schedule of reinforcement. This means that you will no longer be clicking and rewarding at each marker. At first, the transition can be confusing to the horse so rather than going straight into attempting to randomly reinforce him every 1 or 2 markers you may want to start by simply delaying the click a little. For example, if until now you have been clicking every time his shoulders pass the marker, try clicking when his hind passes the marker.

If your horse gets stuck and simply stops at the spot he is expecting the click, try to motivate him to do a few more steps using the target before clicking and treating.

Once you can reinforce every 1 or 2 markers with your horse still circling properly and not getting confused, move on to reinforcing every 2 or 3 markers. Keep going until your horse can at least complete an entire circle without any help or reinforcement.

Step 5: If desired, start fading away the equipment you have been using. So, for example, if you have been using 8 markers so far, rearrange to only use 6 then 4. When fading away the markers pay close attention to how your horse is moving on the circle; if you are using circling to improve the athletic abilities of your horse you may be better off keeping all the markers if removing them affects his performance.

Step 6: If you wish, you could progressively increase the circle size to 20m. The benefit of working on different circle sizes is that the bend in the spine varies accordingly to the size of the circle; the smaller the circle, the more bend is required. It is a good idea to teach your horse to move on a large circle before teaching him to trot on a smaller circle, as it will be less difficult for him to trot on a 20m circle than on 10m one.

8. Teaching your horse to navigate a small figure of eight

In this exercise the horse has to switch between one bend to the other and therefore it can be used to improve suppleness and coordination. This version of the exercise requires little equipment (2 markers and a target stick) and little space but you can also have fun combining it with the circling exercise and ask your horse to move from one large circle to the next.

TRAINING STEPS

Step 1: Place 2 markers at a small distance from each other. Using a target stick guide your horse around the first marker, click while the horse bends around the marker, remove the target and reward. Repeat with the next marker. Do this a few times until the horse is comfortable navigating around the markers.

Step 2: Start fading out the target stick. Use the target to guide the horse towards the marker, remove the target once the horse starts turning, click when he is bending around the marker and reward immediately. Repeat the process several times on both sides before continuing to fade out the use of the target.

You are likely to find fading out the target stick an easier task if you also reinforce the horse for moving from one marker to the next the first few times he does it on his own.

Step 3: Once the horse can do a figure of eight around the markers without needing the target you can change the schedule of reinforcement. So instead of clicking every time the horse goes around a marker, you want to progressively work towards clicking him for completing the entire figure (going around 2 markers).

Héros being guided from one marker to the next using the target stick.

Chapter 6
Trick training

Trick training is often looked down upon by equestrians. Some people may consider tricks a waste of time and some may just go as far as labelling them as degrading to the trainer and/or horse. But what exactly are tricks? From the horse's point of view every operantly shaped behaviour is a trick. There is the "carry the human on your back" trick and the "give your feet" trick; for them there is little difference between these and picking a ball on cue. Humans see things a bit differently; we tend to consider anything that doesn't have an obvious purpose a trick. But what if I told you that tricks taught using positive reinforcement were useful?

The many benefits of tricks:

- Playing games with your horse helps fulfil his need for exploration and play. Fulfilling the needs of your domestic horse is essential if you want your horse to be happy and capable of coping with domestication.

- Stationary or semi-stationary tricks and games are a great way to reduce boredom and the risk of depression in horses that must be stabled to recover from injuries.

- Through classical conditioning, and due to aversive training and handling, horse owners often become a conditioned stimulus that provokes conditioned fear responses in their horses. By taking part in activities that involve pleasurable stimuli instead of fear and/or pain, the association the horse has with his owner can change to a more positive one. Because of this, behaviour such as biting/kicking and running away from the owner can be reduced or extinguished.

- Trick training is a great opportunity for the trainer to refine his training skills.

- During play the horse may offer desired behaviours that you can capture and later on put on cue. For example, you may be able to capture your horse cantering after the ball during a game of football.

1. Teaching your horse to catch

For this game, it is recommended to use protective contact between you and the horse. Having a fence or stable door between you and the horse will allow you to back up to throw the towel without the animal following you.

TRAINING STEPS

Step 1: Present an easy to catch object such as a tea towel to your horse. When the horse touches the towel with his nose, click, remove the towel and reward your horse. Repeat this step several times until he is confident touching the object.

Step 2: Present the towel again but this time do not click when your horse touches it with his nose. When he does not hear the click he will naturally offer something different; chances are he will take the towel between his teeth. When he does, click, remove the towel and reward. Some horses are more shy than others and may simply touch the towel with their lips or lick it; click and reward to encourage the horse to progress towards mouth-based exploration.

Step 3: Once the horse takes the towel between his teeth, you can build up the duration of time the horse must hold the towel by progressively delaying the click and reward.

Left-top picture: steps 2 and 3. Right-top: step 4.
Left-bottom: step 5. Right-bottom: step 6.

Step 4: To introduce your horse to the idea of catching the towel, hold it with two hands so the horse has to bite it by the middle. Move the towel slowly while holding it to get the horse used to having to catch the towel.

Step 5: Once your horse understands the idea, step back and swing the towel towards him while still holding it with one hand. You can start swinging it as slowly as necessary for the horse to succeed. When the horse grabs the towel, you can click and treat.

Step 6: After a bit of practice the horse should be able to catch the towel when you throw it.

2. Teaching your horse to play football

The following training plan explains how you can teach your horse to follow/run after a ball and then either touch it with their nose or kick it.

TRAINING STEPS

Step 1: Start by introducing your horse to a football using nose targeting. While holding the ball in your hand, place yourself at a distance at which the horse is comfortable. Present the ball away from your body and wait for your horse to investigate the object.

Step 2: Click investigative behaviours such as sniffing or touching the ball. Remove the ball and deliver the reward. Repeat several times until the horse confidently touches the ball every time it is presented.

Step 3: Place the football on the ground, click and treat your horse a few times for touching it. Some horses may struggle to touch the ball once you no longer hold it, if this is the case with your horse, start by holding the ball while crouched down and then progress to placing the ball on the ground while remaining crouched. Once the horse has gained confidence progressively raise up to a standing position.

Step 4: If you would like your horse to learn to kick the ball rather than just touching it with his nose, try placing the ball close to his front hooves. When the horse moves his front legs, he will accidentally make contact with the ball. Click the precise moment the horse's hoof comes into contact with the ball and reward. After a few repetitions the horse will seek to kick the ball.

If the horse struggles to make contact with the ball, place the ball near his front hooves and then ask him to move forward into the ball using a target. Keep an eye on the ball and click when he kicks it.

Step 5: Make the task a little bit more difficult this time by placing the ball a couple of metres away from your horse so he will have to take 1 or 2 steps in order to nose or hoof target the ball.

Step 6: Once your horse can move towards the ball + target it, you can kick the ball gently away from your horse and click and reward him for following it and then targeting it with his nose or hoof.

If your horse finds the task difficult or appears to be frustrated by the ball moving away from him, start by reinforcing him for just moving towards it, rather than moving towards it + targeting it.

Step 7: Sometimes during a game you may want to kick the ball toward your horse, this can be scary for some horses therefore you want to get him used to the idea by very gently rolling the ball past him and then click and reward him for intercepting it. Once your horse appears comfortable with the ball being rolled past him, try gently rolling it towards him and click and treat him when he targets it.

Step 8: Now you've got your horse used to the ball going in all directions – away from him, past him and directly toward him – you can start kicking the ball a bit further away.

Step 9: You can also introduce a variable schedule of reinforcement, which means you no longer reinforce every single time he targets the ball. Introduce the new schedule of reinforcement slowly by reinforcing randomly every first time, second time or third time he successfully targets the ball.

If the horse remains calm yet motivated, you can reinforce even less and really focus on providing an external reward for the very best performances only.

If your horse starts to show signs of frustration go back to reinforcing more often or adjust how much of the food reward you give for each click. Big handfuls of low value food rewards are typically better for horses who are easily frustrated as they gain satisfaction from spending more time chewing on the food.

If used properly, a variable schedule of reinforcement can make the game a more exciting and interesting experience. Varying where, and how far away, you throw the ball will also make it more interesting for your horse.

Spirit on his way to nose target the ball.

3. Vocabulary lessons for horses

Equine cognitive abilities are rarely discussed in the equestrian world due to the tendency to solely value horses for what we can do with their bodies. When I started to record and upload videos of my horses partaking in simple discrimination tasks, many people commented "There must be a treat hidden behind the card" or "This horse must be the most intelligent horse I've ever seen". The truth is, there is nothing special with a horse picking a picture of a horse over a picture of a chicken when told "horse" and there is no need to hide a treat behind the desired picture for him to do it. Several studies have proven that horses can discriminate between visual cues, even when rotated (Hanggi, 2010), and can associate specific visuals with corresponding outcomes and use them to communicate preferences to their human caregivers (Mejdell et al, 2016).

Vocabulary lessons are a fun way to practice your training skills and to explore equine cognition. Because they can be conducted in small area and require little movement, they are a perfect way to mentally stimulate horses on box rest.

Here are some suggested tasks for vocabulary lessons:

- Print out 2 drastically different pictures and teach your horse the relevance of 1 of the pictures over the other by giving your horse a food reward for only touching 1 of the pictures.

- Pick up 2 different objects and teach your horse the relevance of 1 object over the other by giving a food reward for only touching/picking up 1 of the objects.

- Complicate the task by adding more objects/pictures and/or rotating the relevant picture/object.

- Using 2 print out images or objects, teach your horse to touch 1 of the items on 1 cue (for example, to touch the picture of a horse when told "horse") and to touch the other item on another cue (for example, to touch the picture of a cat when told "cat").

- Teach colour discrimination using 2 similar objects of 2 different colours. Horses have a dichromatic vision unlike humans who have a trichromatic vision. This means horses see in shades of blues and yellows, 2 colours that they can easily learn to discriminate on cue.

I recommend looking up studies on equine cognition to get inspiration for which stimuli to use and how to set up your lessons. Of course, your aim is not to create scientific data but to have fun with your horse so do not feel discouraged if you don't have the resources to create a flawless procedure.

The following training plan outlines the steps you can take to teach your horse a simple discrimination task made up of 2 symbols. The plan can of course be adjusted to fit your set up.

TRAINING STEPS

Step 1: Print 3 different symbols – including 2 you would like your horse to learn to differentiate between – and a "control" symbol that the horse will not be learning the meaning of. Sticking the symbols to a fence, wall or board of some sort is recommended (but not mandatory) to reduce risk of influencing the horse's decision by holding the symbols yourself.

Step 2: Ensure your horse is comfortable with the surface you plan to stick your symbols on by asking him to approach it and nose target the chosen surface. Click and reward the horse a few times for touching it.

Step 3: Present 1 of the relevant symbols to the horse and click/treat the horse for touching it with his nose a few times before sticking the symbol on the chosen surface. The aim is to make sure the horse isn't afraid of any of the items involved in the lesson.

Step 4: Position 1 of your relevant symbols and give the cue of your choice before allowing the horse to approach and touch the symbol. Click when the horse touches the symbol and then deliver the reward. Repeat a few times until the horse shows no hesitation to approach and precisely touch the symbol.

Step 5: Vary where on the surface you stick the symbol. Your horse should touch the symbol precisely, independently of its position.

Step 6: Introduce your "control" symbol alongside the relevant symbol you have been working on. The first time, make sure to position the relevant symbol right in front of the horse to increase the chance of the horse providing the correct answer. Give your cue and allow the horse to approach and touch the symbol. Ignore the horse's response if he touches the wrong symbol and click/treat when he touches the correct one.

Step 7: Vary the position of the relevant symbol and control symbol and follow the same procedure. The horse is ready to move to the next step of the training when he can correctly identify the relevant symbol 10 times in a row.

In my lesson on colour recognition, I use blue and yellow as my relevant colours – meaning the horse learns to associate these with the corresponding words – and use red as my control.

Step 8: Remove the first symbol and position your other relevant symbol. Give the cue of your choice (it must be different to the one you have used for the first relevant symbol) and allow your horse to approach and touch the symbol. Click when the horse touches the symbol and deliver the reward. Repeat a few times until the horse shows no hesitation to approach and precisely touch the symbol.

Step 9: Repeat steps 6 and 7, this time with the second relevant symbol and the "control" symbol.

Step 10: When the horse can correctly identify the relevant symbols, you can present both relevant symbols together and give the cue of your choice before allowing your horse to approach and select his answer. Just as in step 6, make sure to position the symbol that corresponds to your cue right in front of the horse the first time. If the horse selects the wrong answer ignore it and wait for him to touch the correct symbol to earn a click and a treat. Through trial and error the horse should eventually learn to match the symbol to the cue.

Test your knowledge

This last section is your opportunity to test how much you have learned so far. These questions are only for your benefit so use them however you would like. The quiz can successfully be completed after reading chapter 1 and 2.

Basic learning theory

1. Which quadrant of operant conditioning consists of adding an aversive stimulus following an unwanted behaviour, causing this behaviour to be less likely to occur?

a) Negative reinforcement   b) Negative punishment   c) Positive punishment

2. Which quadrant of operant conditioning consists of removing an aversive stimulus following a wanted behaviour causing this behaviour to be more likely to occur?

a) Negative reinforcement   b) Negative punishment   c) Positive punishment

3. In operant conditioning what does "positive" mean?

a) Good practice   b) Rewarding   c) Adding something

4. By which process can a stimulus gain the capacity to evoke a response that was originally evoked by another stimulus?

a) Operant conditioning   b) Classical conditioning   c) Habituation

5. Which of these prominent psychologists was responsible for the classical conditioning experiment involving dogs?

a) Edward Thorndike   b) B.F. Skinner   c) Ivan Pavlov

Dealing with unwanted and abnormal behaviours

6. What is the first thing you should do if you notice a negative change of behaviour in your horse?

a) Consult your   b) Consult your trainer   c) Nothing
veterinarian

7. Phobias and serious fears in horses can most often be explained by?

a) Operant conditioning   b) Classical conditioning   c) Habituation

8. Which of the following techniques should be avoided when dealing with a fearful horse?

a) Systematic desensitisation   b) Flooding   c) Counter conditioning

9. Which technique consists of exposing the animal to a weaker version of an aversive stimulus in order to increase his tolerance to it?

a) Habituation | b) Systematic desensitisation | c) Counter conditioning

10. What can occur when multiple stressors or stressful events occur at the same time or relatively close together?

a) Generalisation | b) Trigger stacking | c) Saliency

Training desired behaviours

11. In which circumstances it is advisable to use a continuous schedule of reinforcement?

a) When the horse starts to learn a new behaviour | b) For difficult and complex behaviours | c) Continuous schedule should be avoided

12. In which schedule of reinforcement does the trainer reinforce the animal for the first occurrence of the desired behaviour after a fixed time?

a) Fixed ratio | b) Fixed interval | c) Variable interval

13. In clicker training, by which process does an animal learn the meaning of the bridge signal?

a) Habituation | b) Classical conditioning | c) Flooding

14. What's the name of the training technique which consists of guiding the animal into the desired position using a piece of food?

a) Capturing | b) Luring | c) Targeting

15. Which of the following training techniques does not use positive reinforcement?

a) Targeting | b) Free-shaping | c) Pressure-release

Results: 1.c, 2.a, 3.c, 4.b, 5.c, 6.a, 7.b, 8.b, 9.b, 10.b, 11.a, 12.b, 13.b, 14.b, 15.c

Bibliography

Clarke, JV et al. (1996) Effects of observational learning on food selection in horses. Applied Animal Behaviour Science, Volume 50, Issue 2, Pages 177-184

Coleman, K et al. (2010) The use of positive reinforcement training to reduce stereotypic behavior in rhesus macaques. Applied Animal Behaviour Science, Volume 124, Issue 3, pp 142-148

Hanggi, E (2010) Rotated object recognition in four domestic horses (Equus caballus) Journal of Equine Veterinary Science, Volume 30, Issue 4, pp. 175-186

Herron, M et al. (2009) Survey of the use and outcome of confrontational and non-confrontational training methods in client-owned dogs showing undesired behaviours. Applied Animal Behaviour Science, Volume 117, pp 47-54

Hiby, E et al. (2004) Dog training methods: Their use, effectiveness and interaction with behaviour and welfare. Universities for Animal Welfare. 13: 63-69

Hockenhull, J et al. (2010) Unwanted oral investigative behaviour in horses: A note on the relationship between mugging behaviour, hand-feeding titbits and clicker training. Applied Animal Behaviour Science, Volume 127, Issue 3, pp 104-107

Innes, L et al. (2008) Negative versus positive reinforcement: An evaluation of training strategies for rehabilitated horses. Applied Animal Behaviour Science, Volume 112, Issue 3, pp 357-368

Krueger, K et al. (2014) The effects of age, rank and neophobia on social learning in horses. Animal Cognition, Volume 17, Issue 3, pp 645-655

McGreevy, P (2012) Equine Behavior: A Guide for Veterinarians and Equine Scientists. Saunders Ltd.; 2nd edition

Mejdell, C et al. (2016) Horses can learn to use symbols to communicate their preferences. Applied Animal Behaviour Science, Volume 184, pp 66-73

Murrey, N (2007) The effects of combining positive and negative reinforcement during training. Master of science (behaviour analysis)

O'Heare, J & Santos, A (2007). Explaining and changing people's use of aversive stimulation in companion animal training. Journal of Applied Companion Animal Behavior, Volume 1, pp 15-21

Pryor, K. (2006) Don't Shoot the Dog!: The New Art of Teaching and Training. Ringpress Books; 3rd edition

Pryor, K. (2010) Reaching the Animal Mind: Clicker Training and What It Teaches Us About All Animals. Scribner; 1st edition

Sankey, C et al. (2010) Reinforcement as a mediator of the perception of humans by horses (Equus caballus). Animal Cognition, Volume 13, Issue 5, pp 753

Schuetz, A, Farmer, K. & Krueger, K. (2017) Social learning across species: horses (Equus caballus) learn from humans by observation. Animal Cognition, Volume 20, Issue 3, pp 567-573

Zeligs, J. (2014) Animal Training 101: The Complete and Practical Guide to the Art and Science of Behavior Modification. Mill City Press, Inc

Useful links

Visit the author website for free articles: www.fairhorsemanship.com and check out the YouTube channel for useful videos on horse training, behaviour and welfare: www.youtube.com/fairhorsemanship

You can also connect with Alizé on social media using the hashtag #fairhorsemanship

Join the Facebook group "Empowered Equestrians" created by fellow horse trainer Jessica Gonzalez to connect with like-minded horse people.